GETTING AHEAD

DANIEL P. MCMURRER
ISABEL V. SAWHILL

Getting Ahead

Economic and Social Mobility in America

THE URBAN INSTITUTE PRESS
Washington, D.C.

Getting Ahead: Economic and Social Mobility in America/
Daniel P. McMurrer and Isabel V. Sawhill.

Includes bibliographical references and index.

1. Social mobility–United States. 2. Social classes–United States.
3. Family–United States. 4. United States–Social conditions.
5. United States–Economic conditions. 6. United States–Economic
policy. I. Sawhill, Isabel V. II. Title.

HN90.S65M34   1998   97-49260
350.5'13'0973–dc21   CIP

ISBN 0-87766-674-1 (paper, alk. paper)
ISBN 0-87766-673-3 (cloth, alk. paper)

Printed in the United States of America.

Distributed in North America by
University Press of America
4720 Boston Way
Lanham, MD 20706

T his volume began as a series of short essays on various facets of economic and social mobility, a number of which were published during 1996 and 1997 by the Urban Institute, and are reproduced here in a slightly revised form as chapters 2 through 7. Chapters 1, 8, 9, and 10 are new (although they draw, in small part, on an earlier paper published by the Aspen Institute).

We have been deliberately brief so as not to overburden readers who already have much to occupy their attention. But we want the more academically inclined to know that for chapters 4 and 6 we have written longer papers that review the evidence in greater detail. We also believe that intellectual odysseys are never over and view this effort as a way station in a journey we plan to continue in the coming years. We are even more acutely aware of unanswered, or incompletely answered, questions than we were when we began. In that sense, this volume represents an agenda for further work as well as a report on insights gleaned thus far.

We have benefited from the help of numerous individuals who commented on the previously published essays or helped in other ways: Gregory Acs, Benjamin Barber, Laurie Bassi, Daniel Bell, Stephen Bell, Susan Brown, Kathleen Courrier, William Dickens, Maury Gittleman, Arthur Goldberger, Jane Hannaway, Robert Hauser, Robert Haveman, Michael Hout, Thomas Kane, Mickey Kaus, Helen Ladd, Robert Lerman (a coauthor of one of our earlier essays), Frank Levy, Seymour Martin Lipset, Lucy Loewen, Pamela Loprest, Richard Murnane, Demetra Nightingale, Janet Norwood, Donna Pavetti, Deborah Phillips, Bella Rosenberg, Jason Rubenstein, Bradley Schiller, Charles Schultze, Robert Solow, Eugene Steuerle, Christopher Walker, Daniel Weinberg, Douglas Wissoker, and Edward Zigler. Finally, Felicity

Skidmore edited the entire volume cheerfully and expertly, and she and her staff took full responsibility for shepherding it through its final stages.

We want to thank the John D. and Catherine T. MacArthur Foundation for their support of this effort. We also want to thank the Urban Institute, and especially its President, William Gorham, for giving us this opportunity to write about opportunity. One of us had the good fortune to occupy the Arjay Miller chair in public policy at the Urban Institute during this period, making sustained work on this topic possible.

We write this out of a sense of having been given opportunities in the much broader sense as well—opportunities that we would like to see extended to those who have been far less fortunate in their early lives than we have.

Daniel P. McMurrer
Isabel V. Sawhill

November 1997

Contents

Much has been written in recent years about growing income inequality. This book goes behind the facts of income inequality to focus on the determinants of opportunity in America—the fundamental processes that influence who succeeds and who fails.

America has always prided itself on being the land of opportunity—so full of opportunity that everyone has a chance to "make it." But the public debate typically avoids taking a hard look at the validity of that claim. In a culture that prizes equal opportunity rather than equal outcomes, judging how much income inequality is too much demands attention to the underlying determinants of inequality. A society in which everyone has an equal chance to succeed is very different from a society in which some members are not going to succeed, however hard they try. If society decides incomes are "too" unequal, public policy needs to identify and address the root causes, and determine which of them are amenable to policy change.

The authors give cause for both concern and optimism. The slowdown in economic growth over the past few decades has reduced the chances of Americans to realize the traditional American dream—doing better than their parents. But the influence of class—who your parents are—has declined. Greater proportions of Americans than 50 or even 10 years ago now end up on a different rung of the social and economic ladder from that occupied by their parents.

But social origins still influence educational outcomes and, later, economic and social success. What can be done to reduce such inequalities in opportunity? In the authors' view, one of the major culprits—

and certainly the most promising policy focus—is the educational system.

Although education has always been thought of in this country as the great leveler, the current school system actually fosters inequality. As the authors see it, "The failure of schools to impart the knowledge and tools that children need for success in today's labor market puts the heaviest burden on those from disadvantaged families. . . . Their more-privileged counterparts have other sources of learning—their families and communities—which will always give them an edge; but if schools were more effective, these advantages would not loom so large."

The issues surrounding the subject of opportunity are as controversial as they are important—nature versus nurture, equity versus incentives, luck versus effort. *Getting Ahead: Economic and Social Mobility in America* lays out the facts and discusses what research can tell us about possible ways ahead. It is my hope that this discussion will contribute to a public debate which brings us closer to consensus on how to improve access to opportunity for all Americans.

William Gorham
President

Chapter One

Introduction and Overview

The growing gap between rich and poor in the United States has been widely noted. To many, it is alarming and calls for strong action to address what is perceived to be an increasingly bifurcated society in which the most fortunate have prospered while the poor have been left behind. Our thesis is that this single-minded focus on income inequality has led to a preoccupation with what are only the symptoms of a deeper set of forces that badly need to be understood. Where one ends up in the income distribution reflects, after all, where one began, who one's parents were, what kind of education one received, race and gender, and a host of other factors—including just plain luck. Our focus, then, is on what is happening to opportunity—to the process that causes some individuals to be successful while others fail. Understanding what lies behind any particular distribution of incomes very much influences our perceptions of whether that distribution is "good" or "bad" and what, if anything, needs to be done about it. Those who believe that the distribution fairly reflects each person's talents and energies will have one view. Those who believe it is a deck stacked to reward those fortunate enough to have started with the right cards will have another. One cannot judge any particular distribution of incomes without knowing what produced it. Nor can one decide such important questions as whether welfare reform will help or harm poor children, whether educational resources are properly deployed, or whether inheritance taxes are too steep or not steep enough.

Why Focus on Opportunity?

One good reason to focus more attention on opportunity is that Americans have always cared more about equal opportunity than about equal results. The commitment to provide everyone with a fair chance to develop their own talents to the fullest is a central tenet of the American creed. This belief has deep roots in American culture and American history and is part of what distinguishes our public philosophy from that of Europe. Much of that history has revolved around a struggle to level the playing field by reducing discrimination against previously excluded groups and by extending education to an increasingly broad segment of the population. This theme is elaborated in chapter 2, which concludes that substantial progress has occurred on both fronts—to the point where all but 13 percent of the population now graduates from high school and the access of women and minorities to most jobs and educational opportunities has improved dramatically.

Americans' traditional concern about opportunity is only one reason to give it greater attention. Another is that the current emphasis on income inequality begs the question of how much inequality is too much. Virtually no one favors a completely equal distribution of income. It is understood that some inequality in rewards is what drives individual effort and, as such, is essential to economic growth. Many would argue that current inequalities far exceed those needed to encourage work, saving, and risk taking, and that we need not worry about the optimal degree of inequality in a society that has clearly gone beyond that point. But the argument is hard to prove and will not satisfy those who are persuaded that inequality is the price we pay for a dynamic economy and the right of each individual to retain the benefits from his or her own labor. In light of these debates, if any public consensus is to be found, it is more likely to revolve around the issue of opportunity than around the issue of equality.

Still another reason to focus on opportunity is that it suggests a redirection of public policy from treating symptoms to treating underlying causes. As long as inequality of results is perceived to be the problem, a more progressive system of taxes and transfers will seem the logical solution. We do not argue against such progressivity. One should not deny the unfortunate various forms of assistance, but it is obviously better if one can prevent misfortune in the first place. Some argue that giving disadvantaged families more income is the best way to secure more equal opportunities for children. But our reading of the literature on the ability of income transfers per se to accomplish this objective suggests this view may be naive (see chapter 9).

The distribution of income has often been compared to a ladder. Right now, the rungs on the ladder are far apart. Both in comparison to other industrialized countries and to our own past history, the United States has a lot of inequality. We believe a shorter ladder with more closely spaced rungs would be preferable, but our focus in this book is much more on who gets to occupy which rungs. It is not only the distribution of income that should concern us but also the system that produces that distribution. As noted in chapter 3, justice and inequality can be compatible—if the rules that determine who wins and who loses are perceived to be fair. Imagine a society in which incomes were as unequal as they are in the United States but in which everyone had an equal chance of receiving any particular income—that is, in which the game was a completely unbiased lottery. Although some, especially those who are risk adverse, might blanch at the prospect of losing, and might wish for a more equal set of outcomes a priori, others might welcome the chance to do exceedingly well. But no one could complain that they hadn't had an equal shot at achieving a good outcome. So fairness is critical and the rules governing who wins matter more now than in the past precisely because the rewards are so much more unequally distributed. When the stakes are high, when incomes are very unequally distributed, then the way the game is played warrants special scrutiny.

There exists, within the social science literature, a wealth of information on the topic of economic and social mobility—that is, on what determines who gets ahead. In his excellent review of this literature, Robert Haveman notes that this body of work has had far less impact in influencing social policy than might have been expected.[1] Some of the most interesting work was done in the 1960s and 1970s by Christopher Jencks and his colleagues.[2] Jencks's major and somewhat controversial conclusion at the time was that most of the variation in men's incomes had to be ascribed to luck, and that if the public wanted to reduce inequality it would have to redistribute income, not just schooling or early childhood experiences.[3]

Even more controversial than Jencks's work has been the publication of *The Bell Curve* by Richard Herrnstein and Charles Murray.[4] These authors believe that IQ or cognitive ability is both critical to and increasingly important for success. They argue that such ability is largely inherited and that efforts to intervene to ensure better outcomes for the initially disadvantaged are, for this reason, likely to be ineffective. In a curious way and for different reasons, both the Jencks and the Herrnstein-Murray views are pessimistic about our ability to change outcomes by modifying the education system or other early experiences. Jencks's argument is that initial advantages and disadvantages are not that important; Herrnstein and Murray say that they are critical. Jencks would deal with the problem by redistributing income after the fact; Herrnstein and Murray by accepting and then learning to live with inequality. But neither appears to believe it is possible, through public policy, to create significantly more opportunity. Our view is more optimistic. We believe more can be done to increase opportunity.

Whatever their views, both Jencks and Herrnstein and Murray are to be commended for putting these issues on the public agenda. The remarkable fact is how little serious scrutiny they have received outside of the academy. The public may give lip service to the idea of equality of opportunity, but few stop to ask what that should mean in practice and how much of it this country actually has. In particular, too little attention has been given to the critical role played by social origins and inherited ability in determining who ends up where in the distribution of income. Yet it is these deepest of inequalities that have frustrated attempts to provide a greater degree of opportunity. Education is supposed to be the great leveler in our society, but it can just as easily reinforce these initial inequalities. Any attempt to give every child the same chance to succeed has to come to terms with the diversity of both early family environments and inherited abilities and with the need for unequal treatment in favor of the most disadvantaged. Numerous programs—from Head Start to extra funding for children in low-income schools—have been created in efforts to even the playing field. But even where such efforts have been effective, they have been grossly inadequate to the task of compensating for differences in early environment. The result is that the distribution of income is not just unequal. It is, to a greater extent than our public rhetoric would suggest, predictable. The winners and losers are not drawn equally from all sectors of society. In short, understanding the facts about the actual distribution of opportunity is a necessary prerequisite to reshaping the public debate on these issues.

OVERVIEW OF THE REMAINING CHAPTERS

In chapters 2 and 3, we reexamine the country's concern with various inequalities, first in a historical and then in a normative context. In chapter 4, we begin to look at the evidence. We focus first on what is known about how much people move up and down the economic ladder during their adult years. This is sometimes called *intra*generational mobility. In chapters 5 and 6, we focus on *inter*generational mobility—that is, on the extent to which children can, or do, escape their origins by doing better or worse than their parents. In chapter 7, we look at the prospects for upward mobility among the most disadvantaged—welfare recipients, in particular. In chapter 8, we examine the role of the education system in opening up opportunities. In chapter 9, we focus on the reasons why family background is such a strong predictor of adult success. Finally, in chapter 10, we consider the implications of these findings for policy and for the future.

INTRAGENERATIONAL MOBILITY   *(Chapter 4)*

People move up and down the economic ladder throughout their working years. Those at the bottom of the income scale often move up as they accumulate skills and experience, add more earners to the family, or find better jobs. Those at the top may move down as the result of a layoff, divorce, or business failure. Thus, any snapshot of the distribution of incomes in a single year is likely to be a misleading indicator of the distribution of incomes over a lifetime. For example, in a society in which everyone was poor at age 25 but rich by age 55, the distribution of annual incomes would be very unequal but the distribution of lifetime incomes quite equal. This society would be one in which there was a lot of income inequality (as conventionally measured) but simultaneously a lot of opportunity.

Studies of income mobility in the United States suggest that such opportunities do exist. Large proportions of the population move into a new income quintile each year, with estimates ranging from 25 to 40 percent. This evidence indicates that lifetime incomes are indeed more equally distributed than the annual data suggest.

It is also true that income inequality as conventionally measured has been increasing since the late 1960s and that this has not been accompanied by any *increase* in mobility rates. Thus, growing annual income inequality implies growing lifetime income inequality as well.

To return to our ladder analogy, many people move up and down it over the course of their lifetimes. That fact is not in dispute. However, the amount of movement between the rungs has not changed over the past few decades. What has changed is the position of the rungs. They are now farther apart. The distance between those perched at the top and those on the bottom is greater than ever.

INTERGENERATIONAL MOBILITY   *(Chapters 5 and 6)*

Although there is no evidence of increasing opportunities to move up the ladder over one's working life, a rather different story emerges when we turn our attention to what is happening to incomes across generations. Data for the somewhat longer period of time needed to span several generations highlight two important trends that are affecting opportunities for younger generations. On the one hand, they are being negatively affected by a slowdown in the rate of economic growth, which in the past ensured that each generation would have opportunities to move into jobs paying more than those held by their parents. At the same time, younger generations are benefiting from the greater openness of the social structure. Inherited advantages of class play a smaller role now than they used to in shaping the success of individual Americans, with larger numbers now moving beyond their origins. In this sense, opportunity has increased.

The Role of Economic Growth

Young men, born after about 1960, are doing less well than their father's generation did at the same age. In the past, a strongly growing economy guaranteed each generation better economic prospects than the previous one. The growth of the economy has always been an important source of upward mobility, a reason that children tend to be better off than their parents. In a dynamic economy, a farmer's son can become a skilled machinist and the machinist's son the founder of a computer company. Indeed, scholars who have compared the United States to other industrialized countries have discovered that the primary, and perhaps the only, reason for greater mobility in the United States is that, until recently, it experienced faster growth than the older countries of Western Europe. Contrary to popular ideology, it is this economic dynamism rather than any inherent social fluidity or lack of class barriers that is primarily responsible for America's reputation as the land of opportunity. But sometime in the early 1970s, America's economic escalator slowed to a crawl.

The period from the end of World War II to about 1973 was an especially impressive one from an economic standpoint. Productivity grew by 3.0 percent a year between 1960 and 1973. But the good news didn't last. After 1973, productivity growth slowed to 1.1 percent a year. Because the compensation of workers tends to track how much they produce, real wage growth slowed commensurately.

The effects have been felt especially by young men without much education. The combination of slower growth and a distribution of wage gains that have favored women over men and the college-educated over those with high school degrees has left poorly educated men with real incomes that are less than half of what they otherwise would have earned.

More generally, with a slower economic growth rate, it is far more difficult to provide ever-expanding opportunities to each new generation of workers. The youngest generation is discovering this first-hand; young men, in particular, are earning less than their fathers did at comparable ages.

The Role of Class

It is often said that Americans would rather talk about sex than money, but it is also true that they would rather talk about money than class. That class matters in the United States, and matters as much as it does in the older democracies of Western Europe, may come as a surprise to many. But the evidence is clear. Both incomes and occupations are correlated across generations. For example, men with white collar fathers are almost twice as likely as those with blue collar origins to end up in upper white collar jobs. The good news is that class plays a smaller role than it used to in shaping the success of individual Americans. Larger numbers now move beyond their origins. This trend has been evident for at least the last three generations, and one study suggests it dates back to the mid-19th century. It appears to have been driven by the broadening of educational opportunities to more and more Americans, the decline of self-employment where inheritance of a business or a trade may be important, and the increased emphasis on merit in assigning occupational roles. Whatever the reasons, the importance of class in the United States has declined.

Both these factors—the slowdown of economic growth and the declining importance of class—have affected prospects for the youngest generation. The good news is that individuals are increasingly free to move beyond their origins. The bad news is that fewer destinations represent an improvement over where they began. For those concerned about the material well-being of the youngest generation, this is not a welcome message. But for those concerned about the fairness of the process, the news is unambiguously good.

WHAT ABOUT THE UNDERCLASS?   *(Chapter 7)*

Just as Americans have been loathe to believe that class matters in the United States, so too have they resisted the idea that there might be a group of individuals permanently stuck at the bottom of our society with little or no opportunity to improve their lot. Yet research completed in the past decade suggests that such a group may indeed exist. It is concentrated in neighborhoods characterized by high rates of poverty, joblessness, dropping out of school, and single-parent families. Although still relatively small (about three million people in 1990, according to some estimates), it is larger now than it was in 1970.[5]

Many members of this group, and their children, are on welfare. And many of them remain dependent on public assistance for long periods. But with enactment of the Personal Responsibility and Work Opportunity Reconciliation Act of 1996, society's expectations for this group have changed. It is now hoped that most mothers on welfare will find jobs that will enable them to support their families.

We examine the extent to which this hope is likely to be realized and conclude that welfare reform couldn't have come at a better time. With a strong economy, and new welfare rules that require or encourage work, many former or would-be recipients appear to have found jobs or some other means of support. However, it is too early to declare victory. States have not yet had to dig deeply into the more troubled portions of their caseloads. And any faltering of the economy would further undermine their ability to move recipients into the labor market. Among those recipients who do find jobs, the evidence suggests that if they work full time and continue to collect the assistance for which they remain eligible (such as food stamps and the Earned Income Tax Credit), their incomes will be sufficient to move them a bit above the poverty line—depending on family size and availability of subsidized child care. But several recent studies also suggest that these workers are not likely to be upwardly mobile. Most will earn low wages for the balance of their adult years. And the most disadvantaged segments of the current caseload—those most likely to be part of the so-called underclass—may not be capable of even this degree of self-support. Whatever their fate, the real tragedy is the too-frequent inheritance of multiple disadvantages among their children, many of whom seem condemned to repeat their parents' lives.

EDUCATION AND OPPORTUNITY   *(Chapter 8)*

No discussion of social mobility in America would be complete without assessing the role of the education system in opening doors for those from diverse backgrounds. We know that education is more important than ever in today's economy. The most direct evidence of this is the growing wage premium received by those with a college education. But it is also true that mobility, both over the life cycle and across generations, is much greater for those with college degrees. And lack of education is a critical barrier to upward mobility for those at the bottom end of the labor market. In short, education is more than ever the stratifying variable in American life.

The real question, though, is who gets a good education? If education simply reflects the initial advantages of being born into a well-placed family, then it will have limited effects in spreading opportunities through the population. Indeed, it may actually reduce opportunity by certifying these initial advantages.

Research on this question is mixed and open to varying interpretations. Even among those with comparable backgrounds, extra education contributes to later success in the labor market. And to this extent it contributes to opportunity. At the same time, educational outcomes are powerfully influenced by family background, and this influence appears to be growing.

Because schooling is financed largely at the local level, the kind of education a child gets in the United States has always depended on where his parents could afford to live. Buying a house in the right neighborhood—and above all, one with good schools—is the quintessential way of providing a better future for one's children in this country. We examine the extent to which this dependence of schooling on residential location constrains opportunity and conclude that, in general, more money is spent to educate children in more-affluent neighborhoods. We also note that there is no clear association between money spent on education and educational achievement. Still, resources matter—or, more to the point, they should matter. To the extent that they do not, it is an indictment of the effectiveness of the entire system of public elementary and secondary education. The failure of schools to impart the knowledge and tools that children need for success in today's labor market puts the heaviest burden on those from disadvantaged families who, if they are going to learn these skills, are going to learn them in school or not at all. Their more-privileged counterparts have other sources of learning—their families and communities—which will always give them an edge; but if schools were more effective, these advantages would not loom so large. So, inequities in school finance, combined with the general underperformance of the schools, leave less-advantaged children far behind in the competition for good jobs once they reach adulthood.

In addition to its disproportionate impact on the least advantaged, the poor performance of schools has another corollary: the devaluation of a high school diploma and the increased reliance on higher education to signal that one has the competencies needed by employers. Yet it is at the college level that costs to students and parents become most significant and family resources have their strongest effects on access.

We conclude, then, that the rhetorical commitment to equal opportunity in the United States is not matched by a similar commitment to providing all children with a good education.

If there is any public good that should be made an entitlement, and not remain contingent on local fiscal capacity, it is K through 12 education. But providing a more equitable source of financing must be pursued in tandem with reforms that ensure those resources are effectively used. Similarly, providing more access to college through grants, subsidized loans, tax credits, or other means is desirable, but only under two conditions: first, if such assistance is structured in ways that improve student performance at the precollege level, and second, if care is taken to prevent this from fueling a new burst of tuition increases by colleges and universities. Without these safeguards, we will simply end up spending more to provide our youth with the skills that they should have acquired in high school. The most important agenda, however, is to restore the value of the high school diploma itself by improving the performance of students and schools at every level. This conclusion is doubly warranted in an economy that is growing more slowly than in the past and providing its greatest rewards to those with the most skills—making upward mobility even more dependent on education than has been true historically.

WHY FAMILY BACKGROUND MATTERS   *(Chapter 9)*

Despite its importance, no amount of educational opportunity is likely to compensate completely for differences in family background. Social origins will almost surely continue to exert a powerful influence on educational outcomes and later success in the labor market. An obvious question, then, is why is this relationship so strong? What accounts for the fact that children from poorer families do not fare as well later in life as those from more-affluent backgrounds?

In chapter 9, we consider three possible answers. The first is that well-placed parents can pass on advantages to their children without even trying: they have good genes. The second is that they have higher incomes, enabling them to provide better material environments for their children. The third is that they are simply better parents, providing their children an appropriate mix of warmth and discipline, emotional security, intellectual stimulation, and coaching about how to relate to the wider world.

Although it is difficult to disentangle the separate influence of each, we conclude that the role of material resources has probably been exaggerated. Genes clearly matter. We know this from studies of twins or siblings who have been raised apart. However, IQ or other measures of ability are at least somewhat malleable, and differences in intelligence are only a very partial explanation of who ends up where on the ladder of success. Good parenting and an appropriate home environment are much harder to measure but are probably critical, especially during the preschool years.

What Should Be Done?   *(Chapter 10)*

We conclude that improving education—especially preschool and primary education—is critical to realigning American practice with the now-tarnished rhetoric about opportunity. This will require that school resources be more equitably distributed and, at the same time, that these resources be more effectively used. In addition, providing children, including the very youngest infants and toddlers, with an appropriate home environment is key to their later success. Learning does not begin at age five, or even at age three.

We also believe that maintaining the current safety net is important, but note that providing still more income to disadvantaged families may not be the best way to change their children's life chances. Supplementing the incomes of the poor, especially the working poor, may be desirable for lots of reasons—including a sense of fairness—and it may even have some modest effects on child outcomes, but it should not be touted as the primary solution to the problem of unequal opportunity.

Finally, we suggest that all the Sturm und Drang about affirmative action is diverting attention from what should concern us much more—the condition of families and schools in many inner-city neighborhoods. It is these conditions that make it difficult for many children to climb onto even the first rungs of the economic ladder and that add immeasurably to growing social distress in these neighborhoods.

NOTES

1. Robert Haveman, *Poverty Policy and Poverty Research: The Great Society and the Social Sciences* (Madison, Wis.: University of Wisconsin Press, 1987).

2. Christopher Jencks et al., *Inequality: A Reassessment of the Effect of Family and Schooling in America* (New York: Basic Books, 1972).

3. A number of studies suggest that these background variables can explain 20 to 30 percent of the variation in adult incomes, which is hardly inconsequential (see endnote 1 in chapter 9). And the fact that much of the variation in adult success remains unexplained may say more about our ignorance than about the role of pure chance. In his most recent book, *Rethinking Social Policy: Race, Poverty, and the Underclass* (New York: Harper Perennial Library, 1993), Jencks suggests that he may have rethought some of the conclusions in the earlier volume.

4. Richard Herrnstein and Charles Murray, *The Bell Curve: Intelligence and Class Structure in American Life* (New York: Free Press, 1994).

5. Ronald B. Mincy and Susan J. Wiener, *The Underclass in the 1980s: Changing Concept, Constant Reality* (Washington, D.C.: Urban Institute, July 1993). See also Isabel V. Sawhill, "The Underclass: An Overview," *The Public Interest* 96:3–15 (summer 1989).

Chapter Two

Leveling the Playing Field

I n 1931, when the historian James Truslow Adams coined the phrase "the American dream,"[1] he captured something peculiarly American:[2] belief in a society both open and dynamic, grounded in a commitment to individual opportunity and to a better life for each generation. In the American lexicon, as Frank Luntz notes, opportunity "is not just the chance for rapid social mobility, but has also to do with our entrenched belief in the concept of meritocracy. Americans are more likely than [those in] any other democracy to believe that people succeed because of actual individual talents, efforts, and accomplishments rather than the social class into which they are born."[3]

The American dream is now said to be in trouble. Many Americans complain that working hard and playing by the rules no longer ensures the kind of upward mobility that has drawn millions of immigrants to our shores. And many cite the fear that their children's generation will not do as well economically or socially as they have done.

The irony is that these complaints come at a time of unparalleled prosperity and follow a dramatic expansion of opportunities to many previously excluded groups. What has gone wrong? Has opportunity in America really diminished? Or are our expectations as a society simply outstripping what we can achieve?

AMERICAN PUBLIC PHILOSOPHY: A BELIEF IN EQUAL OPPORTUNITY

Most Western European democracies have espoused more egalitarian philosophies than have ever taken root in the United States. American society, instead, has been premised on the idea of equality of opportunity for each individual rather than equality of results. Tocqueville described this attitude as early as the 1830s.[4] It has, if anything, grown stronger over time.[5] Although a progressive tax system and a web of redistributive social programs serve to smooth extreme disparities in the United States, these interventions generally play a smaller role than in most other industrialized nations.

Reflecting an emphasis on establishing a fair process to guide the initial competition rather than on altering the distribution of rewards, public efforts in the United States have been directed toward two goals:

■ Creating a level "playing field," on which all individuals have equal opportunity to seek the rewards of the market economy, regardless of race, sex, nationality, or religion.

■ Equipping individuals with the necessary tools for success on that playing field by broadening access to education.

THE RECORD OF ACHIEVEMENT

Much of U.S. history can be seen as the continuing struggle to achieve these two goals, thereby moving American practice closer to ideology. Benjamin Barber put it this way: "What is perhaps most notable about the American story . . . is how it has worked at every crucial crossroads in our history . . . to capture the aspirations of the excluded and to extend the boundaries of power and property."[6]

The struggle is not over, and the goals are not fully achieved. Progress, nonetheless, has been extraordinary. Legal barriers have come down and attitudes have been transformed. As recently as 150 years ago, almost all African Americans were slaves; women were largely excluded from higher education and the professions, as well as the voting booth; and a large influx of Irish and German immigrants stood near the bottom of the economic ladder.

Today, the earnings of blacks have nearly caught up with those of whites with similar educational backgrounds, and the proportion of young adults who complete high school is now the same for blacks as for whites.[7] In addition, white attitudes have changed dramatically and so has behavior. Although de facto segregation has not disappeared, increasingly blacks and whites live in the same neighborhood, attend the same school or church, and have good friends of the other race. Intermarriage—though still infrequent—has increased dramatically.[8]

Similarly, women are now as well educated as men, enter similar occupations at similar rates of pay, and can swing a national election to a candidate who lacks majority support among men. And finally, numerous immigrant groups have achieved levels of success that often surpass those of other Americans. For example, the incomes of Irish American and German American men now exceed the incomes of men as a group in the United States.[9]

Efforts to extend rights to previously excluded groups have been accompanied by a continuing expansion of educational opportunities. The importance of the education system in creating opportunity has grown as other sources of opportunity have faded. During the 1800s, the vast expanse of unsettled territory was a primary means through which the nation delivered on its promise of a chance of advancement for all citizens, leading Frederick Jackson Turner to deem the West "another name for opportunity."[10] But even then, the common school was viewed as a great leveler and source of upward mobility.[11]

With the closing of the frontier around the turn of the century, Americans increasingly looked to education as the primary source of opportunity. In 1940, Harvard president James Bryant Conant called the public schools a "vast engine" for "regaining that great gift to each succeeding generation—opportunity, a gift that was once the promise of the frontier."[12] The education system expanded dramatically. Between 1900 and 1975, secondary school enrollment increased from 10 percent to over 90 percent among children ages 14 to 17. During the same period, the high school graduation rate increased from 7 percent to 73 percent.[13] College enrollment and graduation rates have also increased significantly.[14]

Today, with technology playing an ever more central role in all industries, the demand for highly educated workers has increased still further.[15] Reflecting this increase, the "wage premium" for education has grown. In 1973, college graduates, on average, earned 45 percent more per hour than high school graduates. By 1995, this differential had increased to 65 percent.[16]

The scale of public spending on education reflects the central role played by education in the United States. While the United States spends relatively little on direct redistributive efforts, it has historically spent more per capita on education than almost any other industrialized nation.[17] Yet most Americans voice support for even more government spending on education. Americans also rank highest in the world in the percentage of citizens who receive higher education, and Americans still remain much more likely than individuals in other countries to support further expansion of higher education opportunities.[18]

DISCONTENTS OF A MERITOCRACY

A society based on equality of opportunity rewards ability and achievement—the dictionary definition of a meritocracy. Historically, the ideal of equal opportunity in the United States has been so grossly compromised by differential treatment of particular groups that much of the nation's political energy has been absorbed by efforts to rectify these injustices. Few have speculated about what society might look like if true equality of opportunity were to be achieved. While that time has not been reached, we have moved far enough to discover that a society based on meritocratic principles is not an unmixed blessing. As the importance of discrimination and illiteracy has faded, other factors—some long overshadowed and others newly emergent—are now playing an increasing role in shaping individual opportunity.

Persistence of Inequality

Progress in eliminating discrimination has not gone hand in hand with reductions in inequality; it has only reshuffled winners and losers in the competition. Many may well have hoped that leveling the playing field would change the distribution of income—a hope that in retrospect was doomed to failure. Changing the rules governing the competition for wealth and status does nothing to change the structure of the market economy and the rewards that flow from it. The degree of inequality is unchanged, even though who ends up where in the income distribution changes.[19]

Psychological Fallout

As access to education or jobs becomes more open, those who do not succeed can no longer point so easily to some external source for their failure.[20] The closer society moves to a level playing field, the more likely it is that the consequences of individual failures will have to be confronted—by society as a whole as well as by the individuals themselves.[21]

Effects on the Family

The leveling of the playing field has liberated women from purely domestic roles. This dramatic change, along with the growth of the welfare state, has undermined the economic basis of marriage. As women have experienced greater job opportunities, their dependence on a husband's earnings and on the institution of marriage has declined. This has led to more divorce, and to more childbearing outside marriage—trends that have been at least partly responsible for the dramatic growth of single-parent families.[22] In the three decades since 1950, the number of children living in single-parent families has increased from 7 percent to 27 percent. This increased incidence of single-parent families, in turn, has had major consequences for the distribution of income and future opportunities for children.

A New Economic Environment

Finally, two economic developments of the last two decades—slowed growth and structural changes that have placed a new premium on skill and education—are threatening the American dream. As long as America was blessed with rapid economic growth, no matter where one was on the economic ladder one could reasonably expect one's children to reach a higher rung. As the growth rate has slowed since the early 1970s, the competition increasingly resembles a game in which one individual can gain only to the extent that another loses. In this environment, where economic growth is not enough to provide all with a ready path up the economic ladder, the opportunity structure matters more, and issues of fairness become more salient.

This conclusion is strengthened to the extent that the rate of growth we experienced in our earlier history was a function of unique factors—such as unlimited access to land and other natural resources in the 19th century, and an inexhaustible world market for our goods in the wake of World War II. It would be nice to believe that we could improve economic opportunities by ratcheting up the growth rate to earlier levels, but no one has yet devised a credible strategy for doing so.

Economic growth has not only slowed, but its benefits now accrue almost entirely to those with the most education. Simply being a loyal, hard-working employee no longer guarantees that one will achieve the American dream. Whatever progress has been made in extending educational opportunities, it has not kept pace with the demand. The fate of the unskilled and the least able in this new environment is a new worry not easily reconciled with existing ideology.

CONCLUSION

America may not yet be a true meritocracy, but opportunity is more equal than it has been in the past. This broadening of opportunity has not produced a more equal distribution of incomes. Indeed, it has produced some new discontents. How one evaluates this mixed record depends very much on some moral understandings and practical policy issues to which we now turn.

NOTES

1. See Robert Samuelson, *The Good Life and Its Discontents* (New York: Times Books, 1995) for more on Adams and the American dream.

2. For a discussion of American "exceptionalism," see Seymour Martin Lipset, *American Exceptionalism* (New York: W.W. Norton, 1996).

3. Frank I. Luntz, "Americans Talk about the American Dream," *The New Promise of American Life*, ed. Lamar Alexander and Chester E. Finn, Jr. (Indianapolis: Hudson Institute, 1995).

4. One should distinguish between American ideology and American practice. Some scholars who have studied the actual degree of social mobility around the time of Tocqueville, using the best available data, find little evidence of a rags to riches pattern. See *Three Centuries of Social Mobility in America*, ed. Edward Pessen (Boston: D.C. Heath & Co., 1974).

5. Lipset (1996), 98.

6. Benjamin Barber, *An Aristocracy of Everyone: The Politics of Education and the Future of America* (New York: Ballantine Books, 1992), 71.

7. Jennifer Day, "Educational Attainment in the United States: March 1995," Report no. P20-489 (Washington, D.C.: U.S. Bureau of the Census, 1996).

8. For a detailed review of black economic progress, see Stephan Thernstrom and Abigail Thernstrom, *America in Black and White* (New York: Simon and Schuster, 1997).

9. Stanley Lieberson and Mary C. Waters, *From Many Strands* (New York: Russell Sage Foundation, 1988), 188.

10. Frederick Jackson Turner, "The Problem of the West," *Atlantic Monthly* (September 1896).

11. See, e.g., James M. McPherson, "The United States at Midcentury," *Battle Cry of Freedom: The Civil War Era* (New York: Oxford University Press, 1988).

12. James Bryant Conant, "Education for a Classless Society: The Jeffersonian Tradition," *Atlantic Monthly* (May 1940).

13. U.S. Bureau of the Census, *Historical Statistics of the United States, Colonial Times to 1970* (1970).

14. For example, the percentage of the population (age 25 and over) with at least a college degree almost tripled between 1960 and 1994 (from 7.7

percent to 22.2 percent). U.S. Bureau of the Census, *Statistical Abstract of the United States 1995* (Washington, D.C.: U.S. Government Printing Office, 1995).

15. Lawrence F. Katz and Kevin M. Murphy, "Changes in Relative Wages, 1963–1987: Supply and Demand Factors," *Quarterly Journal of Economics* 107:35–78 (February 1992).

16. Lawrence Mishel, Jared Bernstein, and John Schmitt, *The State of Working America 1996–97* (Armonk, N.Y.: M.E. Sharpe, 1997), 169.

17. U.S. Department of Education, *Digest of Education Statistics 1996* (Washington, D.C.: U.S. Government Printing Office, 1996).

18. Lipset (1996), 83.

19. Indeed, the erosion of traditional norms about who should hold what jobs at what pay (women should become nurses, not doctors, etc.) appears to have been accompanied by an erosion of social constraints on employer hiring and compensation practices more generally. At the extreme, more open and geographically widespread competition can contribute to the rise of what Robert Frank and Phillip Cook (*The Winner-Take-All Society* [New York: Martin Kessler Books, 1995]) call "winner-take-all" labor markets, which bid up the salaries earned by top performers in a particular field. Those individuals who were previously protected from competition by virtue of being male, white, or the best at whatever they do in their town have been hurt most by these developments. Thus, by loosening the role of social norms and limited spheres of competition relative to the role of supply and demand, the move toward meritocracy may actually increase inequality. White males with little education have been particularly affected.

20. Amartya Sen (*Inequality Reexamined* [New York: Russell Sage Foundation, 1992], 6) notes that the opposite may also occur: "in situations of persistent adversity and deprivation, the victims do not go on grieving and grumbling all the time, and may even lack the motivation to desire a radical change of circumstances."

21. Many commentators have discussed this problem. See, e.g., Daniel Bell, "On Meritocracy and Equality," *The Public Interest,* 43 (1970), and Mickey Kaus, *The End of Equality* (New York: Basic Books, 1992), 47.

22. See, e.g., Andrew J. Cherlin, *Marriage, Divorce, Remarriage* (Cambridge, Mass.: Harvard University Press, 1992), 51–52.

Chapter Three

Defining Social Justice

Americans, as we have seen, are deeply attached to the ideal of equality of opportunity and have made important, if halting, progress toward achieving that ideal. Yet the distribution of income remains more unequal than in other advanced countries and more unequal than 25 years ago.[1]

Liberals believe that this level of inequality is incompatible with economic justice but never define the benchmark against which progress should be measured. Conservatives argue that inequality reflects differences in individual talent and effort, and as such is a spur to economic growth as well as the price we pay for living in a free society. In the words of George Will, there is "no prima facie case against the moral acceptability of increasingly large disparities of wealth."[2] Yet even conservatives have largely accepted a certain amount of redistribution. To quote Will again, large disparities do "not mean that social justice must be defined as whatever distribution of wealth the market produces."

CAN SOCIAL JUSTICE BE DEFINED?

How, then, is social justice to be defined? Would Americans want to live in a society in which incomes were, literally, equal? And, if not, what's the right amount of inequality, and is there too little or too much at present?

As James Q. Wilson notes, evidence drawn from close observation of interactions among young children, from experiments with adult subjects, and from anthropology suggests that notions of fairness are deeply embedded in human nature. Individuals who are otherwise self-regarding and rational will sacrifice their own well-being if it produces what seems to them a fairer distribution of some valued good. Specifically, given a choice between more money for oneself and very little for another versus a smaller sum more equally distributed, individuals regularly choose the latter even when there are no long-lasting ties between the two parties.[3]

It would be naive to suggest that people are entirely altruistic. Those who are fortunate enough to be in the top part of the distribution would like to think they have "earned" the right to be there and that society is better off for their striving. Mixed in with our philanthropic urges is a certain amount of rationalization of position.[4]

To suggest that fairness is either deeply embedded in human nature or a rationalization after the fact does not mean there are no principles or reasoned arguments that can be brought to bear on the topic. We review some of them here.

THREE BASIC QUESTIONS

Tackling the issue of distributive justice requires grappling with three basic questions. First, what does society want to redistribute: What kinds of prizes are at issue? Second, what's the right amount of inequality: How *big* should the prizes be? Third, how open is the process by which individuals compete for these prizes?

The Problem of Value: What Is the Prize?

In thinking about distributive justice, the natural tendency is to focus on income and wealth. Our own treatment of the topic will follow a similar bias. Nonetheless, other outcomes or "goods"—political rights, individual liberties, economic efficiency, and happiness—also matter.[5]

Most of the arguments that plague discussions of social justice ultimately revolve around the weighting of these different values. There is no way, for example, to achieve the kind of egalitarian society that some liberals advocate without intervening in family life to the point of threatening the rights of parents to have and raise children as they see fit—the very integrity of the family as an institution.[6]

Another conflict is the well-known trade-off between equity and efficiency (or between fairness and growth). Redistributing income from wealthy person A to deprived person B may reduce the total size of the pie, because of its effects on the incentives to work of both A and B. Arthur Okun called this the leak in the bucket used to transfer resources from one set of individuals to another. According to the best estimates of economists, transferring a dollar from the rich to the poor can cost society as much as 50 cents in lost total income.[7] The conflict between aggregate efficiency and an equitable distribution of income is very real. Society may have to sacrifice some of its total income to achieve a little more equity or vice versa. That such a trade-off exists may be less surprising than the unwillingness of Americans to accept an increase in the trade-off commensurate with the increase in our affluence.

The Degree of Inequality: How Big Are the Prizes?

Bruce Ackerman asks his readers to imagine a world in which there is only one resource, manna. "When all manna claims are added up, they exceed the available supply. Hence, the question of legitimacy arises, Q asking A why he is entitled to manna that Q also wants."[8] The very phrasing of the question suggests that the burden of proof should be on those who advocate inequality.

John Rawls, whose answer to this question has probably been as influential as any, reasons that the fairest distribution of valued goods is one that individuals would freely choose, or agree to, had they no knowledge of their own ultimate position in society.[9] These include race, sex, social class, even innate talents and psychological propensities. Under such conditions, he postulates that they would only agree to those inequalities that benefited everyone, especially the least advantaged. These can be presumed to be those inequalities required to sustain sufficient effort or call forth sufficient talent in the production of social goods to enable the least advantaged to improve their lot.

The logic of giving special attention to the least advantaged appears to derive from a desire to protect against the worst outcome we can imagine for ourselves. In other words, if we all faced the possibility that we might end up at the bottom of society, we might want to ensure that it was not such a terrible place to be. The assumption is that most of us are a bit risk adverse and would want to avoid a very bad outcome—even if that meant making do with a lot less should we be fortunate enough to end up near the top.

The implications of insisting that the disadvantaged as well as the advantaged gain from any distribution that favors the latter are profound. To see this, imagine a two-person society inhabited by Peter and Paul, who start with equal incomes. Now transfer $1.00 of income from Peter to Paul and assume that this encourages both to work harder, thereby increasing total productivity by enough to leave both better off. How much must total output increase? By more than $1.00 is the answer. Then richer Paul would be able to pay back poorer Peter for the initial transfer and still have something left to share between them.

Put in less abstract terms, any proposal that reduces the taxes of the affluent by curbing the incomes of the poor must more than pay for itself (in terms of increased growth) if it is to meet the Rawlsian test of fairness. Few economists—much less liberal philosophers—believe that such gains are feasible in contemporary society. Equally few believe the converse, that redistributing more income to the poor would make them absolutely worse off. There may be leaks in the bucket, but at the end of the process it is not entirely empty.

Rawlsian conceptions of fairness can be criticized on several grounds. First, it is not at all clear that most people are as risk adverse as Rawls assumes.[10] Second, the process of redistributing income from the more to the less fortunate requires interfering with the basic liberties of those who—for reasons of history, individual effort, or inheritance—happen to begin with certain advantages. As Robert Nozick notes, one cannot simply look at "time-slice principles as constituting the whole story about distributive shares." One must also look at the process that created the distribution and assess the fairness of the process itself. It can be argued that, as long as the process is fair, everyone should be permitted to keep whatever they have earned.[11]

The Fairness of the Process: Who Gets the Prizes?

In a feudal society, whether one is a noble or a serf is ascribed at birth. In the American creed, in contrast, anyone can become president of Microsoft.

Virtually all Americans endorse this vision of an open society, and for many, a belief in its existence is what has made them tolerant of unequal results. What has been left out of the American conversation about opportunity are the facts about how much opportunity there really is.

There are countless articles on the inequality of incomes (Nozick's "time slices"), but very few on the process by which some reach the highest ranks while others are stuck at the bottom. We worry about discrimination against certain racial groups, but not about the role played by family background and inherited ability in determining who gets which prize. Education is supposed to be the great leveler in our society, but it can just as easily reinforce these initial inequalities.

Americans purport to believe in equality of opportunity, but it is not clear that real opportunity is possible unless one is also willing to get rid of the family. Numerous programs from Head Start to extra funding for children in low-income schools have been created in an effort to even the playing field. But even where such efforts have been effective, they have proven grossly inadequate to the task of compensating for differences in family environment.

Even if one were able to offset the effects of family environment, one would be left with differences in inherited ability. What are the implications for opportunity of these differences? The answer depends, of course, on how great one believes those differences to be. The Founding Fathers believed they were relatively small—that "all men are created equal." And Garry Wills's exegesis of 18th-century texts suggests that this was more than just rhetoric,[12] which may help to explain why the creed of opportunity became so deeply rooted in American soil. But Richard Herrnstein and Charles Murray argue that differences in cognitive ability are substantial and largely inherited, that success in today's economy increasingly requires those abilities, and that earnings and social standing will depend to an ever greater extent on inherited differences among people.[13]

One need not resolve the debate about nature versus nurture—and about the ability of social institutions to overcome the effects of both family background and inherited ability—to suspect that these are particularly "deep inequalities," to use Rawls's phrase.[14] Many students of inequality agree. Amartya Sen, for example, believes that any successful attempt to provide real equality of opportunity would have to come to terms with the pervasiveness of human diversity and, thus, the need for very unequal treatment in favor of the disadvantaged. And because these inequalities would continually reassert themselves in each new generation, the intervention would have to be continuous.[15]

A commitment to real equality of opportunity would require a more active public role than is currently found even in the welfare states of Western Europe, and a fortiori, than in the United States. Because the public sector would need to compensate not only for differences in family background but also, and more controversially, for natural ability, it would imply a degree of intervention in the family and in society generally that most Americans would find offensive. It would also place a burden on the public sector that would require it to be much more effective, and more highly esteemed, than it is today. Because liberals have failed to come to grips with the need to compensate for these deepest of inequalities, liberal democracies have produced disappointing results.

Despite various attempts to compensate for early disadvantages, poverty and inequality are still very much with us.

In any case, the issue of process—of exactly how much mobility there is—remains. Justice and inequality can be compatible if the process is a fair one. But until there is greater understanding of the way in which people move up and down the economic ladder, any attempt to find more-effective solutions is likely to further disappoint.

Our thesis about opportunity is that mobility matters and matters more, in some respects, than the distribution of income. The two are linked, however, in an important way. If the distribution of income or other resources in a society is equal, then mobility matters very little. There's almost no place to move to and the prizes or rewards for success are small. But if the distribution is very unequal, then the stakes are much larger and mobility matters more. The bigger the prizes, the more important it is that the competition be a fair one.

At present, in the United States, the prizes are big—bigger, in fact, than they have been at any time since 1968, when inequality in the distribution of income began to increase. So mobility, it seems to us, is particularly salient now. For this reason our next three chapters discuss the evidence on mobility, first in a life cycle context and then across generations.

NOTES

1. Daniel H. Weinberg, "A Brief Look at Postwar U.S. Income Inequality," *Current Population Reports* (Washington, D.C.: U.S. Bureau of the Census, June 1996), reports that the most common measure of income inequality, the Gini index, has increased by over 16 percent since 1968.

2. George Will, "The Great Redistributor," *The Washington Post,* C7 (April 23, 1995).

3. James Q. Wilson, "Fairness," *The Moral Sense* (New York: Free Press, 1993). Quite a different view is taken by some evolutionary psychologists.

4. This tendency of one's thinking to be biased by one's position helps to explain why Republicans have traditionally been the party of the Haves and Democrats the party of the Have-Nots. A recent analysis by Keith Poole

shows that membership in the two major political parties in the United States is increasingly correlated with income.

5. Some scholars have suggested that we have overemphasized the distribution of income and that the focus should be on social democracy in which, regardless of income, there is more mixing of, and mutual respect among, social classes. See Mickey Kaus, *The End of Equality* (New York: Basic Books, 1992); Michael Sandel, *Liberalism and the Limits of Justice* (New York: Cambridge University Press, 1982).

6. This point has been made by Kaus (1992) and is particularly well developed in James Fishkin's *Justice, Equal Opportunity, and the Family* (New Haven, Conn.: Yale University Press, 1983).

7. Robert Haveman, "The Nature, Causes, and Cures of Poverty: Accomplishments from Three Decades of Poverty Research and Policy," *Confronting Poverty: Prescriptions for Change,* ed. Sheldon H. Danziger et al. (New York: Russell Sage Foundation, 1994), 439.

8. Bruce A. Ackerman, *Social Justice in the Liberal State* (New Haven, Conn.: Yale University Press, 1980), 24.

9. John Rawls, *A Theory of Justice* (Cambridge, Mass.: Harvard University Press, 1971).

10. As Peter Passell notes, "Many Americans, it is safe to say, would trade a guarantee of a modest income for substantial opportunity to strike it rich through personal initiative." "The Rich Are Getting Richer, Etc., and It's Likely to Remain That Way," *The New York Times,* D2 (March 28, 1996).

11. Robert Nozick, "Distributive Justice," *Anarchy, State, and Utopia* (New York: Basic Books, 1974).

12. Garry Wills, *Inventing America: Jefferson's Declaration of Independence* (New York: Doubleday, 1978).

13. The logic behind this position was first introduced by Herrnstein, a Harvard psychologist now deceased, in a 1971 article in the *Atlantic Monthly.* It is repeated in Richard Herrnstein and Charles Murray, *The Bell Curve: Intelligence and Class Structure in American Life* (New York: Free Press, 1994), and has been the subject of much commentary, including that by Daniel Bell in his 1972 *Public Interest* article on "Meritocracy and Equality" (1992). Kaus (1992) expresses a view similar to the one we espouse here: namely, that one need not accept the Herrnstein-Murray argument uncritically to believe that they have raised an issue worth worrying about.

14. Rawls (1971), 13.

15. Amartya Sen, *Inequality Reexamined* (New York: Russell Sage Foundation, 1992).

Chapter Four

Moving Up and Down the Economic Ladder

T he half century since World War II can be divided into two periods. In the first period—from 1947 to 1973—family incomes rose at a healthy clip and the gains were more or less equally shared. Between 1973 and 1994, however, incomes rose more slowly and the gains were heavily tilted toward the top of the distribution (chart 4-1).

This part of the story is hardly new. The disappointing rate of economic growth and the growing income gap between rich and poor in recent decades is by now well documented.[1] But there is another chapter in this story.

INEQUALITY AND MOBILITY

Most people would look at the trend depicted in chart 4-1 and conclude that America is becoming a bifurcated society. That is too hasty a conclusion. Although the distribution of income among individuals may be unequal in any given year, this does not necessarily mean it is unequal over their lifetimes. For various reasons, many individuals move up in the distribution over time, while many others move down. And the reasons for movement vary. A poor single mother who marries an accountant, for example, may move up substantially in the year of the marriage. A well-to-do farmer whose crop fails may move way down that year. A young computer programmer who works hard may move up steadily year by year as she acquires more job experience.

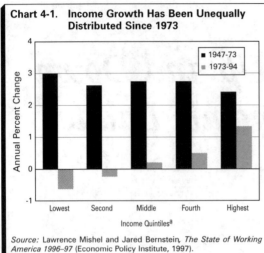

Chart 4-1. Income Growth Has Been Unequally Distributed Since 1973

Source: Lawrence Mishel and Jared Bernstein, *The State of Working America 1996–97* (Economic Policy Institute, 1997).

[a]The lowest income quintile consists of the 20 percent of all families with the lowest income as measured by the Census Bureau. The second quintile consists of the second-poorest 20 percent, and so forth.

Economic historian Joseph Schumpeter compared the income distribution to a hotel—full of rooms that are always occupied, but often by different people.[2] In order to have an accurate picture of an individual's experience over a lifetime, therefore, we must know not only the size of the different rooms but also the rate at which individuals switch rooms.

This switching goes on all the time and makes it difficult to interpret the standard statistics showing how the top (or bottom) 20 percent of the population has fared over some period of time.

Economists now understand that the amount of mobility is just as important as the distribution of economic rewards in any given year, because it determines the extent to which inequality in the short term translates into inequality over the long term. For example, a very unequal distribution of income in any one year would be of little consequence in a society in which individuals were constantly moving up or down the economic ladder, resulting in each receiving an equal share of the rewards over a lifetime. Conversely, a society in which there was very little mobility would have a very different character than the previous one—*even if their annual income distributions looked exactly the same.* Thus, a crucial question is: How much economic mobility is there?

MOBILITY IN THE UNITED STATES

Much less is known about mobility than about inequality. In recent years, however, a number of studies have used survey data to track the incomes of the same individuals over time.[3] The most commonly used technique for analyzing their mobility is to rank their incomes from highest to lowest in a beginning year. Typically, this ranking breaks the sample into five equal-sized groups (quintiles). This is done again for the incomes of these same individuals in a later year. The percentage of individuals who change income quintiles between these two years is then used as an indicator of mobility. Because the focus is on relative position within the distribution, in order for one individual to move up it is necessary for someone else to move down.[4]

How Much Mobility?

These studies of relative mobility have produced remarkably consistent results, with regard to both the degree of mobility and the extent of changes in mobility over time.[5] Mobility in the United States is substantial, according to this evidence. Large proportions of the population move into a new income quintile, with estimates ranging from about 25 to 40 percent in a single year. As one would expect, the mobility rate is even higher over longer periods—about 45 percent over a 5-year period and about 60 percent over both 9-year and 17-year periods.[6]

Who Moves Up?

Which groups are most likely to be *upwardly* mobile in the income distribution? Evidence suggests that, in recent years, individuals with at least a college education are more likely to move up than any other group (chart 4-2).[7] This is a significant change from the 1970s, when income increases were more evenly distributed across educational levels.

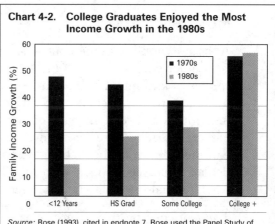

Chart 4-2. **College Graduates Enjoyed the Most Income Growth in the 1980s**

Source: Rose (1993), cited in endnote 7. Rose used the Panel Study of Income Dynamics to calculate growth in real family income, after adjusting for family size, for adults ages 22 to 48 at the beginning of each decade.

International Comparisons

Although mobility in the United States is substantial, evidence indicates that it is no higher in this country than elsewhere. Indeed, the few studies that have directly compared mobility across countries have concluded that, despite significant differences in labor markets and government policies across countries, mobility rates are surprisingly similar.[8]

Other Measures of Mobility

Two widely reported recent studies of mobility in the United States found extremely high rates of mobility—rates that are much higher than those cited above.[9] This results from differences in analytical approach.[10] Most importantly, these studies examined absolute (rather than relative) mobility.[11] Under this definition of mobility, anyone who moves across a fixed threshold (established in the base year or for the population as a whole) is considered mobile regardless of his or her relative position within the distribution. As a result, factors such as economic growth and the natural tendency of incomes to increase with age can cause almost everyone to appear mobile.

Mobility over Time

Although mobility in the United States is neither higher than it is in other countries nor as high (in our view) as suggested by studies of absolute mobility, there is nevertheless broad agreement among researchers that the year-by-year movement of individuals between income quintiles is substantial and that lifetime earnings are more evenly distributed than annual earnings. But what about changes in mobility over time? In particular, what has happened to mobility since the early 1970s, when annual inequality began to increase?

The evidence on this point is clear: Mobility has not changed significantly over the last 25 years. Indeed, a number of different studies indicate that relative mobility rates in the United States—both short term and long term—have been remarkably stable (chart 4-3 displays the results of two out of six mobility studies cited in endnote 5). Thus, Americans continue to move up and down in the income distribution at the same rate as they did in the past.

As a result, the recent increases in annual inequality have proceeded unchecked by any increase in mobility. An individual's income in any one year is always a poor predictor of lifetime income, but it is not a worse predictor now than it was in the past.

Chart 4-3. Mobility Rates Have Not Changed

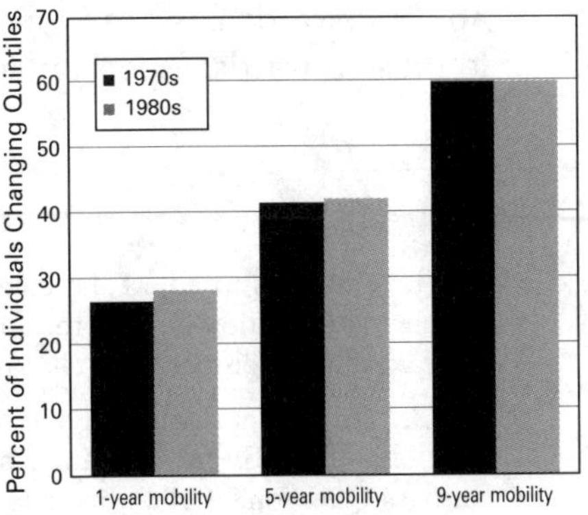

Sources: Data for one-year and five-year mobility are from Burkhauser, Holtz-Eakin, and Rhody (1996), cited in endnote 5; data for nine-year mobility are from Sawhill and Condon (1992), cited in endnote 2. Time periods are slightly different. For one-year and five-year mobility, average rates for 1970–79 and 1980–89 are used; for nine-year mobility, 1967–76 is used for the "1970s" and 1977–86 is used for the "1980s."

Summing Up

The incomes of American families change frequently. Some of the poor get richer, some of the rich get poorer, and for a variety of reasons: accumulation of job skills and experience, marriage and divorce, job change, addition or loss of a second paycheck, and business success or failure.

But despite this churning, overall rates of mobility in the United States have not changed over time. Thus, it is fair to conclude that increases in annual inequality have worsened the distribution of lifetime incomes. Although the disparity in economic rewards has increased, the availability of those rewards—the probability of success or failure—has remained unchanged.

There has been one notable development within this broader picture, however. The mobility of those with little education has declined. Increasingly, a college education is the ticket to upward mobility.

The question of how much inequality is acceptable or appropriate in the United States, as noted earlier, is an issue on which there is no agreement. Still, it is somewhat disturbing to learn that the seemingly relentless growth in the inequality of economic rewards has been unmitigated by any increase in access to those rewards, especially for those with the fewest skills.

NOTES

1. Attempts to adjust the data for changes in family size, for different measures of inflation, for the receipt of capital gains, or for income transfers and taxes have not markedly changed the basic trends described above.

2. For further discussion of this analogy, see Isabel V. Sawhill and Mark Condon, "Is U.S. Income Inequality Really Growing? Sorting Out the Fairness Question," Urban Institute, *Policy Bites* 13 (1992).

3. For a more detailed analysis of these studies, see Daniel P. McMurrer and Isabel V. Sawhill, "Economic Mobility in the United States," Research paper 6722 (Washington, D.C.: Urban Institute, 1996).

4. Thus, if average incomes are increasing over time as a result of economic growth, an individual's income must rise more quickly than the rest of the sample in order to move up to a higher quintile. Movement between quintiles is a relatively crude measure of mobility, as it only roughly captures the magnitude of the change in an individual's income.

5. These studies include Richard V. Burkhauser, Douglas Holtz-Eakin, and Stephen E. Rhody, "Labor Earnings Mobility in the United States and Germany during the Growth Years of the 1980s," mimeograph (Syracuse, N.Y.: Syracuse University, 1996); Mark Condon and Isabel V. Sawhill, "Income Mobility and Permanent Income Inequality," Research paper 6723 (Washington, D.C.: Urban Institute, 1992); Maury Gittleman and Mary Joyce, "Earnings Mobility in the United States, 1967–91," *Monthly Labor Review*, 3–13 (September 1995); Peter Gottschalk, "Notes on 'By Our Own Bootstraps: Economic Opportunity and the Dynamics of Income Distribution,' by Cox and Alm," mimeograph (Boston: Boston College, 1996); Thomas Hungerford, "U.S. Income Mobility in the Seventies and Eighties," *Review of Income and Wealth*, 403–417 (1993); and Sawhill and Condon (1992).

6. Over any period longer than one year, some individual movement between quintiles is not captured by the analysis. For example, an individual who is in the same quintile in both years examined (say, the first and ninth years) may still have moved between quintiles in the intervening years, although he or she would appear to have been "immobile" over the nine-year period.

7. Stephen Rose, "Declining Family Incomes in the 1980s: New Evidence from Longitudinal Data," *Challenge,* 29–36 (November–December 1993).

8. Rolf Aaberge et al., "Income Inequality and Income Mobility in the Scandinavian Countries Compared to the United States," mimeograph, Statistics Norway (1996); Burkhauser et al. (1996); Greg J. Duncan et al., "Poverty Dynamics in Eight Countries," *Journal of Population Economics,* 215–234 (1993).

9. U.S. Department of the Treasury, Office of Tax Analysis, "Household Income Mobility During the 1980s: A Statistical Analysis Based on Tax Return Data" (Washington, D.C.: U.S. Department of the Treasury, 1992); and W. Michael Cox and Richard Alm, "By Our Own Bootstraps: Economic Opportunity and the Dynamics of Income Distribution," *Federal Reserve Bank of Dallas Annual Report 1995* (Dallas: Federal Reserve Bank of Dallas, 1995).

10. For additional discussion of these methodological questions, see Gottschalk (1996) and Paul Krugman, "The Right, the Rich, and the Facts: Deconstructing the Income Distribution Debate," *American Prospect,* 19–31 (fall 1992).

11. Absolute mobility is the movement of an individual in relation to an external standard, usually defined by averages among the population as a whole. Thus, it is possible for all individuals in a fixed group to move up in relation to this external standard. Absolute mobility does not measure change in an individual's relative position within a given sample, and is therefore not comparable to relative mobility.

Chapter Five

Economic Growth and Opportunity

America has always called itself "the land of opportunity." Reality has never quite matched the rhetoric, but a number of factors historically have brought America progressively closer to that ideal. The continued expansion of opportunities to previously excluded groups, the extension of education to an ever-increasing share of the population, and the impressive economic growth that prevailed for many years all made it easier for opportunity to spread broadly through the population.

In recent years, however, this record has not been sustained. The period since the early 1970s has been marked by an unprecedented decline in opportunity for many, especially young men without college degrees. Today, it is more difficult than it has ever been for young workers to surpass their parents' standard of living, thereby achieving the proverbial American dream.

The decrease in opportunity is illustrated by the average earnings of young men. Men born between 1940 and 1949, who were ages 25 to 34 in 1974, had average incomes of almost $30,000 that year (in 1994 dollars). Men born between 1960 and 1969, by contrast, who were 25 to 34 in 1994, averaged less than $23,000 in that year—a precipitous drop (see chart 5-1).[1] Similar trends prevail with regard to family and household incomes,[2] although an increase in the number of two-earner families and growth in fringe benefits have partially offset the effects of the decline in individual wages.[3]

Overall, young men today have lower incomes than their counterparts did in earlier years.[4] This reduction in relative well-being early in the earnings cycle is likely to persist or even worsen as the current generation ages.[5] These economic trends could well have political consequences, as those affected look for someone to blame for their downward mobility.

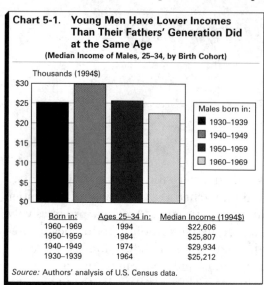

Chart 5-1. Young Men Have Lower Incomes Than Their Fathers' Generation Did at the Same Age
(Median Income of Males, 25–34, by Birth Cohort)

Thousands (1994$)

Males born in:
- 1930–1939
- 1940–1949
- 1950–1959
- 1960–1969

Born in:	Ages 25–34 in:	Median Income (1994$)
1960–1969	1994	$22,606
1950–1959	1984	$25,807
1940–1949	1974	$29,934
1930–1939	1964	$25,212

Source: Authors' analysis of U.S. Census data.

What has gone wrong? Two broad economic trends lurk behind the recent decline in opportunity. First, economic growth has slowed significantly since 1973, causing average earnings to stagnate. Almost simultaneously, earnings inequality has increased, bringing about a dramatic reversal of the trend toward greater equality that had prevailed since World War II. Either trend, occurring alone, would have had troubling consequences. The two trends together have wrought a wrenching change in prospects for many members of the younger generation.[6]

SLOWER ECONOMIC GROWTH

Upward economic mobility and strong economic growth have frequently gone hand in hand. Indeed, in comparing the United States with other countries, some scholars have suggested that the faster rate of economic growth that prevailed in the United States until recently is the primary reason this country enjoyed greater social mobility.[7]

Productivity has increased at an average annual rate of about 2 percent since 1870. The 1960–1973 period saw especially strong growth, with productivity increasing by 3.0 percent per year.[8]

The good news did not last. Productivity slowed to a crawl after 1973—increasing by an average of 1.1 percent per year between 1973 and 1995. Because the compensation of workers tends to track their productivity, real wage growth slowed commensurately.

What is the impact on an average worker of this slowdown in productivity from 3.0 percent to 1.1 percent? Quite a lot. In 1973, the typical male high school graduate could expect an average full-time entry-level wage, in 1995 dollars, of almost $22,000 (see chart 5-2). If productivity had continued to grow at the higher rate of the earlier postwar period, and if this growth had benefited everyone equally, entry-level wages for a male high school graduate by 1995 would have been about $20,000 higher ($42,007). Distributed equally, the actual (slower) growth in productivity, however, would have increased average entry-level wages for these male high school graduates by only about $6,000 from 1973 to 1995.

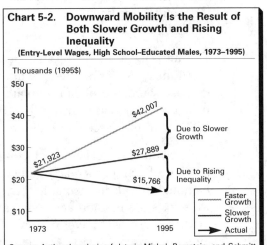

Chart 5-2. Downward Mobility Is the Result of Both Slower Growth and Rising Inequality
(Entry-Level Wages, High School–Educated Males, 1973–1995)

Thousands (1995$)

Source: Authors' analysis of data in Mishel, Bernstein, and Schmitt (1997), cited in endnote 18 of chapter 8.
Note: Fast growth is defined as 3.0 percent per year (actual rate of productivity growth from 1960–1973); slower growth is defined as 1.1 percent per year (actual rate of productivity growth from 1973–1995). Wages are what a full-time, full-year worker would earn at average entry-level wage.

Thus, the slowdown in productivity growth by itself has sharply curtailed the opportunity for the average male high school graduate to improve on standards of living enjoyed by previous generations. Because of the productivity slowdown, his entry-level wages were only slightly higher on average than those of the cohort born 20 years earlier.[9]

INCREASING EARNINGS INEQUALITY

But even this is not the end of the story. An increase in earnings inequality exacerbated the effects of the decline in productivity growth for this group. When rising inequality is also taken into consideration, the entry-level wages for a male high school graduate working full time were under $16,000 in 1995, more than $6,000 *lower* than entry-level wages in 1973. This is over $26,000 less than what would have been expected if the faster growth rate had continued and had benefited everyone equally. Thus, the combined costs to this group of slower growth and rising inequality have been enormous. Each accounts for about half of the $26,000 gap.

The increase in inequality has been documented and analyzed by numerous researchers, who have concluded that wage inequality today is higher than at any time since World War II.[10] It began to increase during the 1970s, surged during the early 1980s, and has since continued to increase.[11]

Males, younger workers, and those who are not college educated have been particularly affected by the combined trends. Although trends in inequality have been the same for men and women, male median earnings have decreased even as female median earnings have increased (in part because of their increased work hours). At the same time, work experience is more highly rewarded by employers than in the past, so younger workers without this experience have also seen a disproportionate decrease in their wages.

Most important, less-skilled, less-educated men have experienced particularly sharp drops in real earnings. In part, this is a result of a significant increase in the pay differential between college-educated workers and others, with college graduates (male and female) earning 65 percent more per hour than high school graduates in 1995, compared with 40 percent more in 1979.[12] The disparity is even greater for entry-level wages, where the wage premium for college graduates was at its peak in 1993 at 77 percent, an increase from 37 percent in 1979.[13]

Most analysts attribute the increased wage differential for education primarily to a substantial increase in the demand for more-educated workers, a shift that appears to have been driven by factors related to technological change. Workers who use computers on the job enjoyed faster wage growth than other workers during the 1980s, which supports this view.[14] Indeed, the forces related to technological change are considered so powerful that they are generally assigned a significant percentage of the responsibility for the overall increase in wage inequality in the United States.[15]

NOTES

1. It should be noted that these numbers slightly underestimate the actual change in total compensation because they do not include fringe benefits, which have constituted a rising proportion of compensation over time.

2. See Lawrence Mishel and Jared Bernstein, *The State of Working America: 1994–95* (Armonk, N.Y.: M.E. Sharpe, 1994), 74.

3. The increase in the number of female-headed households, however, has exacerbated the effects of the wage decline. See, e.g., Robert I. Lerman, "The Impact of the Changing U.S. Family Structure on Child Poverty and Income Inequality," *Economica* 63:S119–S139 (1996).

4. Although average real earnings have declined compared to those of preceding generations, other measures of economic status indicate some improvement for recent generations relative to predecessors. For example, "earnings per adult equivalent," which adjusts for household size, has increased for more-recent generations. This apparent improvement, however, is due primarily to various "demographic adjustments" that have been made by individuals and have had the effect of countering the impact of decreasing earnings. For example, compared to earlier generations, younger adults today are more likely to remain single, marry later, and have fewer children. One study concludes that "this economic success has been purchased at the expense of noneconomic aspects of welfare, such as family life, leisure, privacy, and independence." Richard A. Easterlin, Christine MacDonald, and Diane J. Macunovich, "How Have American Baby Boomers Fared?" *Journal of Population and Economics* 3:287 (1990). See also John Sabelhaus and Joyce Manchester, "Baby Boomers and Their Parents," *Journal of Human Resources* 30:791–806 (1995).

5. See, e.g., Richard A. Easterlin, Christine M. Schaeffer, and Diane J. Macunovich, "Will the Baby Boomers Be Less Well Off Than Their Parents? Income, Wealth, and Family Circumstances over the Life Cycle in the United States," *Population and Development Review* 19:503 (1993), who find that "higher income for a cohort at earlier ages typically foreshadows higher income at later ages." Mishel and Bernstein (1994) find that, in recent years, median family incomes have not only started at a lower income for younger cohorts,

but have also grown more slowly than in the past as the members of the cohorts get older.

6. It should be noted that real wage growth has slowed and inequality has increased in other industrialized nations as well, although the trends have been most pronounced in the United States. See, e.g., Council of Economic Advisers, *Economic Report of the President 1995* (Washington, D.C.: U.S. Government Printing Office, 1995), 172.

7. See, e.g., *America in Perspective*, ed. Daniel Heath (Boston: Houghton Mifflin Co., 1986).

8. Council of Economic Advisers, *Economic Report of the President 1996* (Washington, D.C.: U.S. Government Printing Office, 1996), 332. All productivity statistics reported here are defined as output per hour in the nonfarm business sector, reflect the January 1996 comprehensive revisions of the national income and product accounts, and were computed using chain-type output indices. At this time, revised data are not available for years prior to 1959. Earlier (unrevised) data suggest that the rate of productivity growth that prevailed between the end of World War II and 1959 was slightly lower than the rate between 1960 and 1973.

9. Because this example assumes that the impact of the change in productivity is distributed evenly across the labor force, the preceding two sentences apply to all workers—not only male high school graduates.

10. See, e.g., Frank Levy and Richard J. Murnane, "U.S. Earnings Levels and Earnings Inequality: A Review of Recent Trends and Proposed Explanations," *Journal of Economic Literature* 30:1333–1381 (September 1992); and *Widening Earnings Inequality: Why and Why Now,* ed. Janet L. Norwood (Washington, D.C.: Urban Institute, 1994).

11. Lawrence F. Katz notes that inequality has been found "along essentially every dimension one cuts the [earnings] data and appears to remain no matter how finely one cuts it." Lawrence F. Katz, "Comments and Discussion," *Brookings Papers on Economic Activity* 2:257 (1994).

12. Lawrence Mishel, Jared Bernstein, and John Schmitt, *The State of Working America 1996–97* (Armonk, N.Y.: M.E. Sharpe, 1997).

13. Mishel and Bernstein (1994), 140–147.

14. Alan B. Krueger, "How Computers Have Changed the Wage Structure: Evidence from Microdata, 1984–1989," *Quarterly Journal of Economics* 108:33–60 (February 1993).

15. Gary Burtless, "International Trade and the Rise in Earnings Inequality," *Journal of Economic Literature* 33:815n.11 (June 1995).

Chapter Six

Class and Opportunity

Americans are more likely than individuals in other nations to believe in the importance of talent and effort in shaping a person's life prospects. They are also more likely to reject social class as an acceptable determinant of whether someone succeeds or fails.[1] Given such a strong consensus on the goal of equal opportunity, the American public has paid remarkably little attention to how close society is to achieving it.

Evidence suggests that family background matters quite a bit—that this society is still far from providing everyone an equal chance to succeed. At the same time, real progress has been made. Inherited advantages of class play a smaller role than they used to in shaping the success of individual Americans, with larger numbers now moving beyond their origins. In this sense, opportunity has increased.

But in another sense, it has not. In the past, the dynamism of the U.S. economy ensured that each generation's prospects were better than those of the last one, irrespective of social origins. Almost all Americans were able to achieve more than their parents. As economic growth has slowed in recent decades, however, so has opportunity. The depressing effect of this growth slowdown has almost completely offset the opportunity gains that have come from the declining importance of class.

CLASS STILL MATTERS

Opportunity is here defined as the extent to which an individual's economic and social status is determined by his or her own skills and effort rather than by class of origin. It is typically measured as the relationship between parents and their offspring[2] on various indicators of class—occupational status and income are common ones.[3] The more closely the status of individuals reflects the status of their parents, the less opportunity exists in a society and the more class matters. Conversely, the more independent the overall parent-offspring relationship, the less class matters.

In today's America, the socioeconomic class into which individuals are born significantly affects their status as adults. Even in an open, fair, and dynamic society, of course, some relationship between the status of parents and their adult children would be expected.[4] Genetic inheritance alone is likely to account for some of this (although estimates suggest that it would be an extremely small fraction). Further, there will always be a tendency for parents who occupy positions of high status—whether through their own achievements or for other reasons—to try to extend their advantages to their children. This is a tendency for which public policy can probably never fully compensate as long as children are reared within their own families. Thus, it is almost impossible to imagine a society in which parents' and children's outcomes are completely independent.

The link between the incomes and occupations of parents and offspring in the United States, however, is stronger than would be expected even given these considerations. Recent studies have found an observed correlation between the incomes of fathers and sons of about 0.4.[5] This means, for example, that an adult son whose father's income was a quarter of the way from the bottom of the income distribution (at the 25th percentile) would have a 50 percent chance of having an income in the bottom two-fifths (chart 6-1). Conversely, a son whose father's income was at the 95th percentile (not shown) would have a 76 percent chance of being above the median, including a 42 percent chance of being in the top 20 percent.

Occupations are similarly correlated across generations, with children of professionals significantly more likely to become professionals as adults, and children of blue collar workers significantly more likely to work in blue collar occupations (chart 6-2). For example, men with white collar origins are almost twice as likely as those with blue collar origins to end up in upper white collar jobs.

Thus, origins continue to matter. Children from advantaged backgrounds are likely to do well as adults, and children from disadvantaged backgrounds are more likely to do badly. But this is not the end of the story.

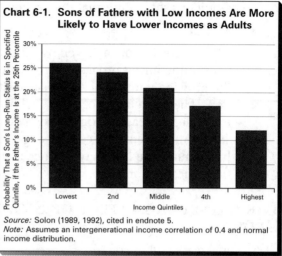

Chart 6-1. Sons of Fathers with Low Incomes Are More Likely to Have Lower Incomes as Adults

Source: Solon (1989, 1992), cited in endnote 5.
Note: Assumes an intergenerational income correlation of 0.4 and normal income distribution.

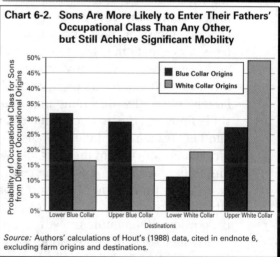

Chart 6-2. Sons Are More Likely to Enter Their Fathers' Occupational Class Than Any Other, but Still Achieve Significant Mobility

Source: Authors' calculations of Hout's (1988) data, cited in endnote 6, excluding farm origins and destinations.

CLASS MATTERS LESS THAN PREVIOUSLY

Class may still matter in the United States, but not as much as it used to. The effect of parents' occupational status on that of their offspring declined by about one-third in less than a generation, according to one study.[6] Other studies have confirmed this decline and have shown that it is a continuing one, evident for at least the last three generations and probably longer.[7] One ambitious study finds that the decline dates back to the mid-19th century.[8]

The decline has been driven by the growth of meritocratic practices in the hiring process, the decline of self-employment, and the growing number of Americans with access to higher education. The percentage of adults who are college graduates, for example, increased from 8 percent in 1960 to 23 percent in 1995. Attainment of a college degree has been shown to greatly attenuate the link between occupational origins and occupational destinations.

The Offsetting Effect of Slower Economic Growth

As discussed in chapter 5, the vigorous economic growth that fueled continuing change in the occupational structure of the U.S. economy for most of our history has declined, slowing the pace of occupational change along with it. The economy itself is no longer creating as many chances for individuals to move up the economic ladder as used to be the case—a trend that has largely offset the declining importance of background. One study finds that the two trends have almost completely offset one another, resulting in little overall change in the rates at which individuals move from the class into which they were born.[9] The only difference has come in the composition of upward mobility. A larger proportion of upward mobility across generations is attributable to the declining importance of class and a smaller proportion to economic growth (chart 6-3). (If individual opportunity increases in an economy that is not growing at all, intergenerational churning between the socioeconomic classes will increase, but there may be no net improvement for younger generations over their parents.)[10]

This change in the composition of upward mobility—growing individual opportunity and lagging economic growth—is important, because it will be felt differently by different groups, depending on where they start. Everyone is hurt by slower growth. But individuals from more-modest backgrounds will benefit from a more open, less class-based social structure. On balance, according to the data, they should come out ahead. For individuals from more-privileged backgrounds, in contrast, the increased individual "opportunity" implied by the declining importance of class represents an increased likelihood of moving down the social scale. They are more likely than before to experience a drop in status relative to their parents. Both trends (economic growth and individual opportunity) represent losses for them.

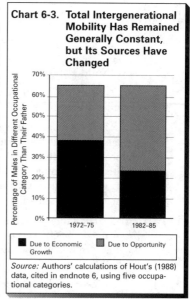

Chart 6-3. **Total Intergenerational Mobility Has Remained Generally Constant, but Its Sources Have Changed**

Source: Authors' calculations of Hout's (1988) data, cited in endnote 6, using five occupational categories.

SUMMING UP

The United States remains a society in which class matters. Children who grow up in privileged families are more likely to become highly paid professionals, for example, than are children raised in less-advantaged households. Still, the effects of family background have declined in recent years. Success is less likely to be inherited than it was in earlier years, suggesting that the American playing field is becoming more equal.

The role of higher education in increasing individual opportunity is notable. Educational attainment in the United States has improved significantly, suggesting that opportunity may continue to grow as a result.

The failure of the economy to grow as rapidly as in the past is equally notable, however. Even as individual opportunity has increased, the slowing of economic growth and the related stagnation of occupational prospects have almost offset this gain. While individuals are increasingly free to move from their roots, fewer destinations represent improvements.

NOTES

1. See, e.g., Seymour Martin Lipset, *American Exceptionalism* (New York: W.W. Norton, 1996).

2. Because of data limitations, many of the studies in this area have excluded women, focusing on the relationship between fathers and sons.

3. To analyze income relationships, researchers compare the incomes of parents (frequently only fathers) at a certain age with the incomes of their children at a similar age. Analysis of occupational relationships is more complicated. This comparison also requires ranking occupations on a hierarchical scale, which is usually based on a combination of the average income and average years of schooling associated with each occupation.

4. For a more complete discussion of how much opportunity might exist in an open society, see Daniel P. McMurrer, Mark Condon, and Isabel V. Sawhill, "Intergenerational Mobility in the United States," Research paper 6796 (Washington, D.C.: Urban Institute, 1997).

5. Gary Solon, "Intergenerational Income Mobility in the United States," *American Economic Review* 82:393–408 (1992); Gary Solon, "Intergenerational Income Mobility in the United States," Discussion paper no. 894-89 (Madison, Wis.: University of Wisconsin Institute for Research on Poverty, 1989); and David J. Zimmerman, "Regression toward Mediocrity in Economic Stature," *American Economic Review* 82:409–429 (1992).

6. Michael Hout, "More Universalism, Less Structural Mobility: The American Occupational Structure in the 1980s," *American Journal of Sociology* 93:1358–1400 (1988).

7. Timothy Biblarz, Vern Bengston, and Alexander Bucur, "Social Mobility across Three Generations," *Journal of Marriage and the Family* 58:188–200 (1996). See also David Grusky and Thomas DiPrete, "Recent Trends in the Process of Stratification," *Demography* 27:617–637 (1990).

8. David Grusky, "American Social Mobility in the 19th and 20th Centuries," Working paper no. 86-28 (Madison, Wis.: University of Wisconsin Center for Demography and Ecology, 1989).

9. Hout (1988).

10. Different rates of fertility can also affect overall levels of mobility. If less-privileged individuals reproduce more rapidly than the more privileged, more people will be able to experience upward mobility—even in the absence of economic growth.

Chapter Seven

Opportunity for Low-Wage Workers

O ne measure of opportunity in any society is its ability to provide jobs for everyone who wants to work. This issue is most
urgent for would-be workers at the low end of the skills, and
wage, distribution. To give some specificity to our discussion, we focus
on the job and earning opportunities available to the increasing numbers of poorly educated job seekers being thrust into the low-wage
labor market by the newest wave of welfare reform. Opportunity in
this arena depends not only on job availability but also on the ability
to compete for available jobs and on the chances of ever earning
enough to be self-sufficient.

ARE JOBS AVAILABLE?

With the unemployment rate in late 1997 at its lowest level in 24 years,
it is hard to argue that jobs are not available. The economy has been
generating an average of almost two million new jobs a year since
1983, and the proportion of working-age adults in jobs has reached an
all-time high. In the process, millions of new entrants—including baby
boomers, immigrants, and women returning to work—have been
absorbed into the labor force.

The pace of job creation has been particularly strong in recent years.
Between April 1993 and April 1997, the economy generated almost
10 million new jobs, allowing the unemployment rate to fall from

7.1 percent to 4.8 percent even as the number of persons working or looking for work was growing by 6 percent. This job growth has benefited everyone, including the poorest, the least educated, and the least skilled.[1] Welfare reform, in short, could not have come at a better time.

But how many new workers are there likely to be in total because of welfare reform, and can the economy absorb the influx? Our analysis suggests the new law is likely to add over 800,000 new workers between 1997 and 2002—roughly 140,000 per year, on average (see chapter appendix for details). Compared to the projected growth of the labor force over this same period—which, at 1.4 million a year, is more than 10 times as great—140,000 is a relatively small addition. And if the demand for workers continues to grow as rapidly as it has over the last decade (about 2 million per year), the economy can easily produce a sufficient number of jobs to accommodate welfare recipients or other low-skilled workers entering the labor force.[2]

Even if the entry of these new workers is not accompanied by any adjustment in total demand for workers (to accommodate the new influx)—so that all of those entering the labor force as a result of welfare reform remain unemployed (or displace other workers into joblessness)—the overall unemployment rate will rise by less than a tenth of a percentage point each year (one-half a percentage point cumulatively over six years).[3] In particular areas of the country, the task of absorbing recipients into the local labor market will be more challenging, however, because the ratio of recipients to jobs is much higher in some communities than others.[4]

If and when the economy enters a recession, of course, the picture will change. The number of jobs will grow more slowly, if at all, and depending on how states react, more people will become jobless or the welfare rolls will swell or both.[5]

WILL WELFARE RECIPIENTS BE ABLE TO COMPETE FOR THE AVAILABLE JOBS?

Even if plenty of jobs are available, new entrants with few skills and little exposure to the world of work will not necessarily be able to compete successfully with other workers for these jobs. The likelihood is that some will find jobs, whereas others will not.

One piece of evidence suggesting that many recipients are employable is the sharp drop in caseloads between January 1994 and January 1997. Almost one million recipients disappeared from the rolls. We do not know for sure how many actually found jobs—some may have already had jobs that they had not reported to the welfare system, some may have turned to other sources of income, some may simply have become poorer[6]—but the strong implication is that a greater reliance on work was at least part of the story for these individuals.

To be sure, much of this decline in welfare receipt can be attributed to the expansion of the economy and only confirms what has long been known. Strong labor markets create opportunities for everyone, including the least skilled. However, new welfare rules at the state level (which include more work requirements, tougher sanctions for not complying with these requirements, and time limits for welfare recipients) have also contributed to the drop.[7] These rule changes have discouraged people from coming onto the rolls as well as encouraged those already on to leave.

So, the experience of the past few years suggests that—when pulled by a strong economy and pushed by new welfare rules— at least some of the unskilled can find work.

The bad news is that those who remain on welfare are going to be an increasingly disadvantaged group, made up disproportionately of those least likely to succeed in the job market. Once the more job-ready recipients have found work, states will have to dig deeper into the caseload, where they will find a higher proportion of persons who are sick, addicted to alcohol and drugs, or functionally illiterate.[8] Pressure to push these hard-to-employ individuals into jobs—which is already substantial because of the new law—will become even greater as they begin to exceed the five-year federal time limit on welfare receipt.[9] States will then need to choose between supporting such individuals with their own funds or pushing them into a job market where they are more likely to sink than swim.

These very disadvantaged recipients may be unable to find a job—any job. Employment opportunities for unskilled workers in some areas are limited, and even where such opportunities exist, employers are not willing to hire those who do not meet certain minimum standards. For example, some inner-city residents report difficulties in obtaining even entry-level, minimum-wage jobs in the fast food industry, while inner-city employers simultaneously complain that they cannot find qualified applicants even for jobs that require relatively few skills.[10] Tight labor markets may cause employers to relax their hiring standards, but cannot entirely solve this problem.

Overall, then, welfare reform is likely to have mixed effects. Many welfare recipients appear to be finding work in today's strong economy, but others will almost certainly encounter serious difficulties. The cumulative effect will depend in large part on the state of the economy and on the success of efforts to train and place low-skilled workers in available jobs. Such efforts have had only modest success in the past, but at the margin they can make a difference.[11]

Welfare recipients are not the only ones who will be affected by welfare reform. Other low-skilled workers will face greater competition for available jobs and may suffer increased joblessness as well. In addition, the increased competition for jobs is almost certain to depress earnings at the low end of the scale.

HOW MUCH WILL THE JOBS PAY?

Studies that have examined the earnings of those who were, at one time, on welfare provide some insight into the likely earnings prospects of current welfare recipients. They suggest that former welfare recipients earn $7.00 to $8.00 per hour (in 1996 dollars) during their first year after exiting welfare and receive, on average, very low annual wage increases. (Table 7-1 summarizes the study results.[12] Even though the numbers have been adjusted to account for the recent decline in real earnings for low-wage workers, they may still overstate the earnings prospects of current welfare recipients. This is because those who went to work in the past did so voluntarily and were probably more job-ready than many current recipients.)

If former recipients were to work full-time, year-round at these wage rates, their earnings would be between $14,000 and $16,000, which is higher than the 1996 poverty line of $12,600 for a mother with two children. Actual annual earnings for such workers, however, are significantly lower than the poverty line, due to the low number of hours worked by such mothers. Their actual earnings are typically between $9,000 and $12,000 (or between 70 and 95 percent of the poverty line).[13]

The earnings of low-wage workers are often supplemented by other government programs, notably the Earned Income Tax Credit (EITC) and food stamps. For example, a mother with two children who earned $10,000 per year in 1996 (slightly less than a full-time, year-round worker would earn after the new minimum wage of $5.15 per hour is fully implemented) would also qualify for $3,556 from the EITC and about $2,400 in food

Table 7-1. Earnings of Current or Former AFDC Female Recipients, Various Studies and Years

Study	Data Source	Sample	Actual Wage Rate/Earnings (1996 Dollars)[a]	"Potential" Earnings If Working Full-Time, Year-Round (1996 Dollars)
Burtless (1995)	National Longitudinal Survey of Youth	Received AFDC sometime between 1979–81 and had earnings	$7.00/hour in 1979 $7.77/hour in 1990 $4,538/year in 1980 $11,575/year in 1990	$14,000 in 1979 $15,540 in 1990
Harris (1996)	Panel Study of Income Dynamics	Exited welfare sometime between 1983–88, estimated earnings	$8.00/hr at exit $7.78/hr after 12 mo. $7.74/hr after 24 mo. $8.04/hr after 36 mo.	$16,000 at exit $15,560 at 12 mo. $15,480 at 24 mo. $16,080 at 36 mo.
Meyer and Cancian (1996)	National Longitudinal Survey of Youth	Received AFDC between 1979–87 and had earnings	$6,087 1st year after exit $9,900 5th year after exit	N/A

Sources: Authors' calculations, based on references cited in endnotes 12 and 13.
a. Real earnings for female workers at the 20th percentile of the earnings distribution (which are roughly comparable to the earnings of former welfare recipients, based on analysis of AFDC recipients and workers at 25th percentile in Burtless 1995, 80) declined at an annual rate of 0.3 percent between 1989 and 1995 (Lawrence Mishel, Jared Bernstein, and John Schmitt, *The State of Working America 1996–97*, Washington, D.C.: Economic Policy Institute, 1997). We adjusted earnings for this annual rate of decline, and then adjusted them for inflation.

stamps. Payroll taxes would reduce earnings by $765. All told, such a worker would have a total income of just over $15,000—before child care and other expenses and after the deduction of the payroll tax (chart 7-1).[14]

Thus, former welfare recipients who are able to find full-time, year-round employment are not likely to be poor. However, child care expenses or the need to reduce hours of work in order to provide such care oneself complicate the picture. On the assumption that former recipients pay the average $3,000 per year in child care expenses incurred by single mothers who work,[15] the incomes they would have available to spend on other needs would fall below the poverty line. For mothers able to get subsidized care, incomes would be commensurately higher.

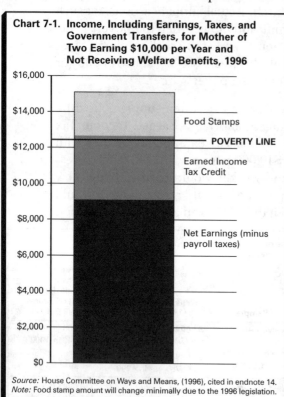

Chart 7-1. Income, Including Earnings, Taxes, and Government Transfers, for Mother of Two Earning $10,000 per Year and Not Receiving Welfare Benefits, 1996

- Food Stamps
- POVERTY LINE
- Earned Income Tax Credit
- Net Earnings (minus payroll taxes)

Source: House Committee on Ways and Means, (1996), cited in endnote 14.
Note: Food stamp amount will change minimally due to the 1996 legislation.

HOW DIFFICULT WILL IT BE TO MOVE UP THE JOB LADDER?

The long-term prospects of those on welfare will depend on their ability to move up the economic ladder. Many workers in low-wage jobs do indeed move up into steady and better-paying employment, often do so relatively rapidly, and usually remain in a good job thereafter.[16] This suggests that significant opportunities to move up continue to exist in the low-wage labor market as a whole, although there are signs that this upward mobility is declining.[17]

Many former welfare recipients, however, are likely to encounter difficulties in taking advantage of these opportunities.[18] Although many workers in low-wage jobs do move up the economic ladder, another large segment of low-wage workers remains in such jobs for extended periods with little or no increase in pay. The characteristics of these workers resemble those of many former welfare recipients, as they are disproportionately less educated, female, and minority.

Thus, opportunities to move up continue to exist for some workers in the low-wage labor market, but they may be becoming more narrowly available. And many former welfare recipients who do succeed in obtaining low-wage work may have particular difficulty moving up the job ladder.

NOTES

Robert I. Lerman contributed to this chapter.

1. Between 1993 and 1995 (the most recent available data), household income growth was greatest for the lowest fifth of the income distribution. Council of Economic Advisers, *Economic Report of the President 1997* (Washington, D.C.: U.S. Government Printing Office, 1997).

2. There have been only three years since 1980 when employment didn't increase by at least one million new jobs per year.

3. The potential impact on the unemployment rate from welfare recipients entering the labor market was calculated by applying the following official projections: (1) the Office of Management and Budget (OMB) projects that the unemployment rate, if there had been no welfare reform, would have been 5.5 percent in 2002 (OMB, *Analytical Perspectives: Budget of the United States Government* [Washington, D.C.: U.S. Government Printing Office, 1997]), and (2) the Bureau of Labor Statistics projects that the labor force growth rate, if there had been no welfare reform, would have been 1.1 percent annually through 2005 (Howard N. Fullerton, "The 2005 Labor Force: Growing, but Slowly," *Monthly Labor Review*, 29–44 (November 1995).

4. For example, in the middle of 1996, the ratio was about 1 percent in Indianapolis, 4 percent in the District of Columbia, and 9 percent in New York City.

5. Former welfare recipients who have gained sufficient previous job experience will be eligible for unemployment insurance. At the same time, it is likely that the complex new welfare formulae would actually require states to *increase* the number of welfare recipients moving into the labor force during a recession. See Daniel P. McMurrer and Isabel V. Sawhill, "Planning for the Best of Times," *The Washington Post,* A19 (August 18, 1997).

6. A recent study by Mathematica Policy Research ("Iowa's Limited Benefit Plan," 1997) found that, among workers in Iowa who had been cut off the welfare rolls, most individuals found some way—either through informal means of support such as family or friends, or through legal or illegal work—to make ends meet. About half reported incomes higher than or equal to their welfare benefits, while the other half experienced a decrease.

7. The Council of Economic Advisers (CEA) finds that almost one-third of the decline is related to these state rule changes. CEA, "Explaining the Decline in Welfare Receipt, 1993–1996" (Washington, D.C.: The White House, May 1997).

8. Krista Olson and LaDonna Pavetti, *Personal and Family Challenges to the Successful Transition from Welfare to Work* (Washington, D.C.: Urban Institute, 1996).

9. Up to 20 percent of the caseload may be exempted from the five-year federal time limit, at state option.

10. Katherine Newman and Chauncy Lennon, "Finding Work in the Inner City: How Hard Is It Now? How Hard Will It Be for AFDC Recipients?" Working paper no. 76 (New York: Russell Sage Foundation, 1995); and Harry Holzer, *What Employers Want* (New York: Russell Sage Foundation, 1996).

11. Robert LaLonde, "The Promise of Public Sector–Sponsored Training Programs," *Journal of Economic Perspectives* 9:149–168 (1995); Larry L. Orr et al., *Does Training for the Disadvantaged Work? Evidence from the National JTPA Study* (Washington, D.C.: Urban Institute Press 1995); Dan Bloom, *After AFDC: Welfare-to-Work Choices and Challenges for States* (New York: Manpower Demonstration Research Corporation, 1997); and Demetra Smith Nightingale, "Work-Related Resources and Services: Implications for TANF," *New Federalism: Issues and Options for States,* A-7 (Washington, D.C.: Urban Institute, April 1997).

12. These data are for individuals who had earnings. They are drawn from Gary Burtless, "Employment Prospects of Welfare Recipients," *The Work Alternative: Welfare Reform and the Realities of the Job Market,* ed. Demetra Smith Nightingale and Robert Haveman (Washington, D.C.: Urban Institute Press, 1995), who studied 10 years of wage rates and earnings for women who had

received AFDC sometime between 1979 and 1981; and from Kathleen Mullan Harris, "Life after Welfare: Women, Work, and Repeat Dependency," *American Sociological Review* 61:407–426 (1996), who studied three years of wage rates for women who exited welfare sometime between 1983 and 1988.

13. Earnings estimates are based on data from Burtless (1995); Daniel R. Meyer and Maria Cancian, "Life after Welfare: The Economic Well-Being of Women and Children Following an Exit from AFDC," Discussion paper no. 1101-96 (Madison, Wis.: University of Wisconsin Institute for Research on Poverty, 1996); and Mathematica Policy Research (1997), which finds weekly earnings of $170 (or $8,840 if year-round) for individuals in Iowa who were recently cut off of benefits. All data are for workers with earnings, and are reported in 1996 dollars after adjusting for declines in real earnings for low-wage workers over this period. See table 7-1 for more details.

14. House Committee on Ways and Means, *Overview of Entitlement Programs: 1996 Green Book,* 104th Cong., 2d sess., 1996, WMCP 104-14, 399. The food stamps estimate does not take into account changes in the food stamps law, which will have only minimal effects on the level of benefits for this worker in 1997.

In addition, many welfare families will be able to draw on housing assistance or child support payments or both. The *1996 Green Book* reports that, in 1994, about 30 percent of AFDC households received housing benefits averaging about $2,650 per year. Further, although only about 5 percent reported receiving child support while on AFDC, improved incentives to obtain child support, more-efficient procedures to establish paternity, and tougher enforcement tools are likely to increase the role of child support as an income source for employed former welfare recipients.

15. Calculated in 1996 dollars, using average expenditures for single mothers and assuming 40 hours of child care per week. Sandra Hofferth, April Brayfield, Sharon Deich, and Pamela Holcomb, *National Child Care Survey, 1990* (Washington, D.C.: Urban Institute, 1991), 136.

16. See Ralph Smith and Bruce Vavrichek, "The Wage Mobility of Minimum Wage Workers," *Industrial and Labor Relations Review* 46:82–88 (1992); Congressional Budget Office (CBO), "In Pursuit of Higher Wages and Employment-Based Health Insurance," memorandum (Washington, D.C.: CBO, 1993); and LaDonna Pavetti and Gregory Acs, "Moving Up, Moving Out, or Going Nowhere? A Study of the Employment Patterns of Young Mothers and the Implications for Welfare Reform" (Washington, D.C.: Urban Institute, 1997).

17. For example, earnings are rising more slowly for low-wage workers as they gain experience. See Rebecca Blank, "Outlook for the U.S. Labor Market and Prospects for Low-Wage Entry Jobs," in Nightingale and Haveman (1995).

18. See Burtless (1995).

APPENDIX TO CHAPTER SEVEN

How Many New Workers Will Welfare Reform Add to the Labor Force?

Under the new welfare law, states are likely to put increasing pressure on recipients to leave welfare for work for at least three reasons: (1) the difficulties of serving a potentially growing caseload with a fixed-dollar federal block grant; (2) requirements that states place an increasing proportion of eligible recipients in approved work activities (which include taking a job); and (3) a five-year time limit on federally funded assistance for any individual.

Most attention has focused on time limits. However, states can always choose to use federal monies to support short-term recipients, freeing up their own funds to support individuals on the caseloads longer than five years. If most states choose this option, the other two factors—generalized fiscal pressures associated with the block grant and increasingly stringent work requirements—are likely to have even more influence on state efforts to move recipients toward self-sufficiency.

The work provision mandates that 25 percent of eligible recipients in one-adult families participate in approved work activities in 1997. The required percentage increases by 5 percentage points each year, reaching 50 percent by 2002. Participation requirements among two-parent families are significantly higher—75 percent in 1997, increasing to 90 percent in 1999 and thereafter. The financial penalties for failing to meet these requirements are significant and the political costs may be even greater.

Meeting such stringent work requirements would be very difficult for most states if it were not for a provision of the law that counts any decline in a state's welfare caseload since fiscal year 1995 toward the participation requirement. Although states are not allowed to change eligibility rules to meet their targets, they can make other changes—such as instituting tougher work requirements for individual recipients, imposing sanctions for noncompliance with these or other requirements, imposing shorter time limits, or taking other measures that will ensure that fewer people apply for, or remain on, welfare.

Because welfare caseloads have already declined by 800,000 households since 1995, most states are expected to meet their work participation targets for 1997—at least for single-parent families, who make up 90 percent of the nonexempt caseload. The challenge for future years will be to either reduce caseloads or increase enrollments in work activities by about 5 percentage points more each year. Either way, most of those so affected will represent net additions to the labor force and will count toward meeting the targets.[a]

Assuming that (1) the average fiscal year 1997 monthly caseload falls to 4.0 million and then increases slowly in later years and (2) all states just meet the participation requirements for both types of families, our calculations indicate that net additions to the labor force will average 139,000 additional workers per year, or a total of 832,000 workers over the six years from 1997 to 2002. The impact on the labor market is likely to be highest in the first year (due in good part to the stringent participation requirement for two-adult families). If some states do better than their targets and hardly any do worse, the net annual increases would exceed 139,000. Conversely, if a number of states fail to meet the targets—which is most likely to happen for the two-parent family requirements—the number would be lower.

a. Because a large proportion of welfare recipients are already working but not reporting it to the authorities, some of the additions to the workforce will be "statistical" rather than "real." Kathryn Edin and Laura Lein, *Making Ends Meet* (New York: Russell Sage Foundation, 1997), 181, estimate that up to 40 percent of welfare recipients work without reporting it (although not all of these individuals are working sufficient hours to count as "working" under the new welfare law).

Chapter Eight

Education and Opportunity

T he education system, particularly public education, has always been viewed as the primary engine for achieving a fair and equal chance to get ahead, regardless of family background. The United States spends more per capita on education than do most other industrialized nations,[1] and most international comparisons of educational attainment (years of schooling completed) rank the United States at the top.[2] In 1996, over 87 percent of 25- to 29-year-old Americans had completed high school, up from 75 percent in 1970 and 61 percent in 1960.[3] Yet despite this broad availability of educational opportunity, family background continues to play a substantial role in determining individual economic success.[4]

There are two likely explanations for this, both of which call into question the widely held belief that our current education system levels the playing field and creates opportunities for Americans from widely diverse backgrounds. The first is that the elementary and secondary education system does not do a very effective job of compensating for the "deeper inequalities"—those arising from differing family backgrounds and circumstances. The second is that higher education—the education level that is now most dependent on one's background—is playing an increasingly important role in determining success.

THE STRUCTURE AND RECORD OF ELEMENTARY AND SECONDARY EDUCATION

Education expenditures in the United States totaled 7 percent of gross domestic product in 1996, up from 5 percent in 1959. Per-pupil expenditures have also increased, suggesting increased emphasis on education over time. Of the $529 billion spent annually in the United States for education, 80 percent of it public spending, $318 billion is spent on elementary and secondary education and $211 billion for higher education.[5]

What is the impact of these expenditures on opportunity? At the most fundamental level, education increases individual opportunity by developing skills that are rewarded in the labor market. The extent to which these skills are actually developed depends on numerous factors, including a student's abilities and efforts, teachers' competence, parents' willingness to assist and encourage their children, and the school resources available to be tapped by students and teachers. Many of these factors are either directly or indirectly shaped by a student's family background.

Thus, education plays a dual role. It can enhance an individual's opportunity and upward mobility, but it can simultaneously serve as a vehicle through which advantages or disadvantages are passed from parents to children. In order for the school system to create more opportunity, its opportunity-enhancing role must be greater than its status-retaining role.[6] Research has consistently shown, however, that its status-retaining role is substantial.

As early as 1966, the Coleman Report found that the characteristics of schools had little effect on student achievement independent of social background. As a result, "the inequalities imposed on children by their home, neighborhood, and peer environment are carried along to become the inequalities with which they confront adult life at the end of school."[7] A classic study by Jencks six years later reached the same general conclusion: family matters much more than any other factor.[8]

The same is true today. Even a brief examination of the current relationship between standardized test scores and various measures of family background confirms the powerful influence of background on student ability and achievement. Scores on tests such as the SAT increase consistently as family income increases (chart 8-1). In 1996, students from families with incomes between $40,000 and $50,000, for example, had average combined SAT scores that were more than 140 points higher than those for students from families with less than $10,000 in income.[9] Achievement tests such as the National Assessment of Educational Progress (NAEP) show similar results for the influence of parental education. In 1994, the average mathematics score for 13-year-olds who had at least one parent who had graduated from college was 285, while the comparable score for students whose parents had less than a high school education was 30 points lower. Similar patterns prevail across other NAEP subjects and other age groups.[10]

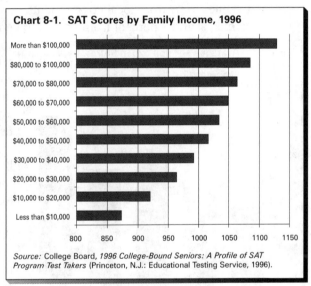

Chart 8-1. SAT Scores by Family Income, 1996

Source: College Board, *1996 College-Bound Seniors: A Profile of SAT Program Test Takers* (Princeton, N.J.: Educational Testing Service, 1996).

Among the many reasons for the strong relationship between students' achievement as measured by standardized test scores and their socioeconomic background, several are difficult or impossible for public policy to affect, including home environment, ability, and parental expectations. But two influences are amenable to policy change: (1) the distribution of school resources and (2) the system's effectiveness in translating those resources into improved student achievement.

School Finance

If education is truly to be a leveling force, it is not enough that its benefits be distributed equally. They must be distributed progressively—that is, children from less-advantaged backgrounds must gain more from education than those who are more advantaged. The current method of financing schools is inconsistent with this goal.

In the United States, most funds for the public schools are raised through local property taxes (although the proportion varies significantly by state). In 1994, 48 percent of all public school revenues came from local governments, 45 percent from state governments, and 7 percent from the federal government. As a result, spending on students is typically higher in wealthier than in poorer districts. In 1992–1993, average per-pupil expenditures for students in districts with median household incomes of more than $35,000, for example, were 27 percent higher than expenditures for those students in districts with median household incomes below $20,000 (chart 8-2).[11]

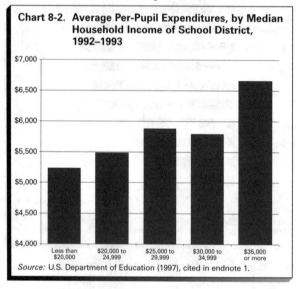

Chart 8-2. **Average Per-Pupil Expenditures, by Median Household Income of School District, 1992–1993**

Source: U.S. Department of Education (1997), cited in endnote 1.

Such averages can mask even larger differences in per-pupil spending, both in comparisons between districts in the same state and across states. In some states, the difference between per-pupil expenditures for districts at the 5th percentile of the distribution and those at the 95th percentile can be as high as $5,000.[12] Even so, almost two-thirds of all measured inequality results from funding differences between richer and poorer states. New Jersey, for example, spends almost two-and-a-half times as much per student as Alabama.[13]

Despite the magnitude of these disparities, there is no consensus on whether school resources affect outcomes such as test scores and labor market success—an issue that continues to be intensely debated among researchers.[14] The very existence of this debate, however, points to a crucial conclusion. Money should matter. A good education system should be defined as one that can transform additional resources into improved student outcomes. Otherwise, why spend money on schools? Thus, the uncertainty about whether outcomes are in fact driven by resources is a symptom of a further problem—the poor performance of the schools. Given current inequities in school finance, if schools are *not* transmitting initial advantages and disadvantages across generations, this can only be because the education system is not performing very well.

And regardless of the effectiveness of the system, the unequal distribution of resources makes it clear that the current method of school finance in no way compensates for differences in family background. To the contrary, if financing inequalities have any effects at all on student outcomes, they favor those from more-advantaged families.

Educational Performance

As the debate over the effects of school resources on student achievement suggests, schools have not been able to translate additional resources into improved performance in recent decades. Per-pupil expenditures increased by 83 percent between 1970 and 1994. At the same time, student-teacher ratios dropped by 22 percent, and the percentage of teachers with a master's degree almost doubled.[15] Despite these increases in resources and associated educational inputs, student scores on the NAEP (the "nation's report card") over the same period have been relatively constant, with a slight decrease in performance over the first half of the period and a slight increase over the second half. A large majority of students still fail to reach "proficient" status, and many do not meet even "basic" performance levels.[16]

Educational inefficiency disproportionately hurts students from disadvantaged backgrounds. By the very nature of their backgrounds, these students are the most dependent on education as the primary vehicle for developing the skills that they will need to succeed in the labor market. Students from more-advantaged backgrounds are more likely to have alternative sources of support and instruction, such as their family or community. So, even if the effects of educational inefficiency are distributed equally across different types of schools (e.g., urban versus suburban), the very existence of that inefficiency reduces the education system's capacity to compensate for the deeper socioeconomic differences that limit opportunities for disadvantaged students.[17]

THE INCREASING ROLE OF HIGHER EDUCATION

Partly because of its inefficiency, the system of elementary and secondary schools in the United States has been unable to keep up with an increasing demand for skilled workers, driven largely by the growing importance of technology in the workplace. One result has been an increase in the role of the higher education system in determining individual economic success. The rewards for individuals with more education have increased relative to those with less: the wage premium paid to workers with a college degree relative to those with a high school degree, for example, increased steadily between 1979 and 1995, from 27 percent to 44 percent for men, and from 31 to 52 percent for women.[18]

Many of the skills that are in increasing demand, however, are not ones that require a college education. Indeed, at least one study has found that a substantial portion of the growth in the college–high school wage gap simply reflects employer demand for strong basic skills—regardless of whether the skills were developed in high school or college.[19] The problem is that employers are reluctant to accept a high school diploma as evidence of adequate skills—further evidence of inefficiency in the elementary and secondary schools. It is thus left to the higher education system to provide many of the skills required for success in today's economy, as well as to provide meaningful credentials for students who have developed those skills. For such basic skills to be provided at the college level is a poor use of scarce educational resources—which could be devoted to other purposes if such skills were more effectively taught earlier in a student's career.[20]

THE INFLUENCE OF SOCIOECONOMIC BACKGROUND ON HIGHER EDUCATION

The influence of family background on educational attainment continues—indeed, is even stronger—at the higher education level. It affects the likelihood that a student will enroll in college, the type of institution attended, and the likelihood of completing a degree. Among 16- to 24-year-old high school graduates in the top fifth of the family income distribution in 1995, the percentage enrolling in college in the fall after high school graduation was 83 percent, compared with 56 percent for those in the broad middle and only 34 percent for students in the bottom fifth.

Comparisons with earlier data reveal that these differences have increased significantly over time, driven primarily by increases in the likelihood of college enrollment among those from higher-income families.[21] High school graduates from families with incomes in the top fifth of the distribution were 30 percent more likely to enroll in college in 1995 than in 1979, while those from families with incomes in the lowest fifth were only 10 percent more likely to do so.

This relationship between college attendance and family background holds true *even when controlling for achievement.* Chart 8-3 tells the story for 1994, not in terms of family income but in terms of another measure of socioeconomic status (SES), which includes characteristics such as parents' education and parents' occupation in addition to family income. Over 95 percent of the highest achievers from high-SES backgrounds went to college within two years of high school graduation versus 77 percent of the highest achievers from low-SES backgrounds. Indeed, these high achievers from low-SES backgrounds were no more likely

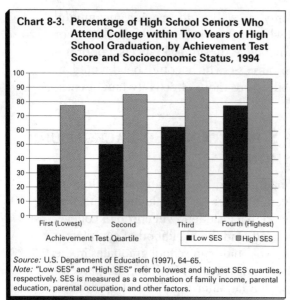

Chart 8-3. Percentage of High School Seniors Who Attend College within Two Years of High School Graduation, by Achievement Test Score and Socioeconomic Status, 1994

Source: U.S. Department of Education (1997), 64–65.
Note: "Low SES" and "High SES" refer to lowest and highest SES quartiles, respectively. SES is measured as a combination of family income, parental education, parental occupation, and other factors.

to make it to college within two years of graduation than the *low* achievers from high-SES backgrounds.[22]

Given that college tuition increases have far outpaced the rate of inflation in the economy as a whole, the increasing effect of family background on college enrollment is not surprising.[23] The tuition increases have made it ever more difficult for students from disadvantaged families to afford college tuition—particularly at many of the four-year private institutions—without significant public or private assistance. Recently enacted tax credits designed to offset higher education expenses may help somewhat in this regard, but they may also further inflate the cost of college.

At the same time, probably as a result of those very tuition increases, students from wealthier families are enrolling more and more in the more-affordable public universities[24]—increasing the competition for spaces in these public institutions. Thus, disadvantaged students face pressure from two sides: increasing tuition at already hard-to-afford private colleges and universities, and increased competition at many public institutions.

Even when the difference in the likelihood of attending college is ignored and attention is restricted to those who actually enroll in college, the influence of family background continues to be powerful. It affects who graduates: in 1994, among students who had enrolled in college five years earlier seeking a bachelor's degree, 53 percent of those from families in the top quarter of the socioeconomic scale had received a bachelor's degree, compared with 39 percent from the families in the middle and 22 percent from families in the lowest quarter.[25]

Thus, family background has a significant and increasing effect on who goes to college, where, and for how long. With the rewards for going to college greater than ever, and family background now a stronger influence over who reaps those rewards, the United States is at risk of becoming more class stratified in coming decades.

NOTES

1. U.S. Department of Education, *The Condition of Education 1997* (Washington, D.C.: U.S. Government Printing Office, 1997), 176–177.

2. For example, the United States has the highest level of average educational attainment across the entire population and also the highest rate of completion of higher education (almost 25 percent of 25- to 29-year-olds had completed four or more years of college in 1995). U.S. Department of Education (1997), 96–7.

3. U.S. Department of Education, *Digest of Education Statistics 1996* (Washington, D.C.: U.S. Government Printing Office, 1996), 17.

4. For additional discussion of this topic, see chapter 6.

5. U.S. Department of Education (1996).

6. It is not clear which role is larger. One piece of evidence comes from a classic study by David Featherman, "Opportunities Are Expanding," *Society* 16:4–11 (1979), which found that education, independent of social background (i.e., the opportunity-enhancing component of education), explains about 20 percent of variation in occupational achievement and that the overlapping influence of social background and education (i.e., the status-retaining component) explains about 14 percent of the variation. See discussion in Robert Haveman, *Poverty Policy and Poverty Research: The Great Society and the Social Sciences* (Madison, Wis.: University of Wisconsin Press, 1987), 114n.9.

7. James S. Coleman et al., *Equality of Educational Opportunity* (Washington, D.C.: U.S. Government Printing Office, 1966).

8. Christopher Jencks et al., *Inequality: A Reassessment of the Effect of Family and Schooling in America* (New York: Basic Books, 1972).

9. College Board, *1996 College-Bound Seniors: A Profile of SAT Program Test Takers* (Princeton, N.J.: Educational Testing Service, 1996).

10. National Center for Education Statistics, *NAEP 1994 Trends in Academic Progress* (Washington, D.C.: U.S. Department of Education, 1996), 64.

11. U.S. Department of Education (1997), 170. See also Thomas B. Parrish, Christine S. Matsumoto, and William J. Fowler, *Disparities in Public School District Spending: 1989–90* (Washington, D.C.: U.S. Government Printing Office, 1995).

12. Wayne Riddle and Liane White, "Expenditures in Public School Districts: Estimates of Disparities and Analysis of Their Causes," U.S. Department of Education, *Developments in School Finance 1996* (Washington, D.C.: U.S. Government Printing Office, 1996).

13. This comparison does not take into account differences in costs of living across states, which would reduce the disparity somewhat. William N. Evans, Sheila E. Murray, and Robert M. Schwab, "Schoolhouses, Courthouses, and Statehouses after *Serrano*," *Journal of Policy Analysis and Management* 16:10–31 (1997).

14. Some have interpreted the evidence to mean that variations in expenditures are not reflected in differences in student performance on standardized tests (Eric A. Hanushek, "The Economics of Schooling: Production and Efficiency in Public Schools," *Journal of Economic Literature* 24:1147–77 [1986]; and Eric A. Hanushek, "School Resources and Student Performance," ed. Gary Burtless, *Does Money Matter?* [Washington, D.C.: Brookings Institution, 1996]). Others interpret the evidence on test performances differently (Larry V. Hedges and Rob Greenwald, "Have Times Changed? The Relationship between School Resources and Student Performance," in Burtless [1996]) or argue that such analyses are inappropriate for analyzing the question of whether money matters (Richard Murnane, "Interpreting the Evidence on 'Does Money Matter?'" *Harvard Journal on Legislation* 28:457–464 [1991]). Still others examine the effects of expenditure differences on labor market earnings, rather than test scores, and conclude that there is a positive effect (David Card and Alan B. Krueger, "Does School Quality Matter? Returns to Education and the Characteristics of Public Schools in the United States," *Journal of Political Economy* 100:1–40 [1992]; and David Card and Alan B. Krueger, "Labor Market Effects of School Quality: Theory and Evidence," in Burtless [1996]). Finally, others have recently suggested that one primary effect of increased school expenditures has been a decrease in class size—and that smaller classes have had a significant positive effect on achievement among minority and low-income students (David Grissmer, A. Flanagan, and Stephanie Williamson, "Changing Families, Schools, Communities, and Public Investment: Can They Explain the Increase in Black Test Scores?" ed. Christopher Jencks and Meredith Phillips, *The Black-White Test Score Gap* [Washington, D.C.: Brookings Institution, forthcoming]). See introductory chapter of Burtless (1996) for a summary of this debate.

15. U.S. Department of Education (1996), 74, 77. See Hanushek (1996) for a more detailed argument about the "collapse of productivity" in the public schools.

Caution should be exercised in interpreting the growth in spending and decrease in student-teacher ratios. These trends can be explained in part by the growth of special-education programs. For example, the percentage of students served in federally supported programs for specific learning disabilities more than tripled between 1976–77 and 1993–94 (U.S. Department of Education [1996], 65). Further, other trends (such as an increase in the percentage of children living in single-parent households and the increase in the number of children living in poverty) have also made the schools' jobs more difficult.

It should also be noted that there is a continuing debate over the proper method of adjusting for inflation in school spending. This adjustment has a significant effect on the measurement of school spending over time. See Richard Rothstein and Karen H. Miles, "Where's the Money Gone? Changes in the Level and Composition of Education Spending" (Washington, D.C.: Economic Policy Institute, 1995); Richard Rothstein and Lawrence Mishel, "Alternatives for Deflating Education Expenditures over Time," U.S. Department of Education, *Developments in School Finance 1996* (Washington, D.C.: U.S. Government Printing Office, 1996); and Hanushek (1996) for further discussion.

16. National Center for Education Statistics (1996).

17. Many believe that school districts that contain significant numbers of disadvantaged children (frequently, large urban districts) are, on average, less efficient than other districts. And anecdotal evidence often supports this belief. Simple aggregate data, however, suggest that the distribution of inefficiency may not be as disproportionate as many believe. For example, data indicate that there are few differences across districts in expenditure patterns, as districts with large percentages of children in poverty are similar to other districts in the percentage of their funds that they devote to expenditures for instructional purposes (see U.S. Department of Education [1997], 307). Again, however, such districts would have to be more efficient than other districts in order for education to be able to act as a progressive force in society. Of that, there is little evidence.

18. Lawrence Mishel, Jared Bernstein, and John Schmitt, *The State of Working America 1996–97* (Armonk, N.Y.: M.E. Sharpe, 1997), 169–70.

19. Richard J. Murnane, John B. Willett, and Frank Levy, "The Growing Importance of Cognitive Skills in Wage Determination," *Review of Economics and Statistics* (1996), 251–266. For additional discussion of this subject, see Richard J. Murnane and Frank Levy, *Teaching the New Basic Skills* (New York: Free Press, 1996).

20. Some, such as Thomas Kane of Harvard University, have suggested that the community college system represents an efficient alternative instrument for developing the necessary basic skills in students who have emerged from the elementary-secondary system without such skills. Average costs per student in community colleges are similar to those in elementary-secondary education (although opportunity costs are higher for adult students, who are out of the labor force). Further, due to the wide variety of such schools, course offerings may be more flexible and may be better tailored to the needs of certain types of students—such as those who failed to develop necessary skills in high school.

21. U.S. Department of Education (1997), 62–63; and Stephen V. Heckman and James J. Cameron, "The Dynamics of Educational Attainment for Blacks, Hispanics, and Whites," conference presentation at the American Enterprise Institute, "Financing College Tuition: Government Policies and Social Priorities," Washington, D.C., May 16, 1997.

22. U.S. Department of Education (1997), 64–65.

23. For further discussion, see Thomas Kane, "Rationing College," conference presentation at the American Enterprise Institute, "Financing College Tuition: Government Policies and Social Priorities," Washington, D.C., May 16, 1997.

24. Michael McPherson and Morton Schapiro, *The Student Aid Game: Meeting Need and Rewarding Talent in American Higher Education* (Princeton, N.J.: Princeton University Press, 1998).

25. U.S. Department of Education (1996), 318.

Chapter Nine

Why Families Matter

I n several previous chapters, especially chapter 6, we have noted the importance of family background to later success, whether in school or in the labor market. In this chapter, we delve a little further into just how important it is and why.

HOW IMPORTANT IS FAMILY BACKGROUND?

As stressed in chapter 6, family background or class is important. (The term "family background" can be defined in different ways. It is most commonly understood to mean the economic and social status of the family in which one grew up, as measured by the income, occupation, and/or education of one or both parents. But the definition can be expanded to include parents' marital status, number of siblings, race, residential location, and other descriptors of early environment.)

Although most studies find that family background matters, its effects should not be exaggerated. It cannot explain more than 20 to 30 percent[1] of the variation in an individual's economic status as an adult. This should not be surprising. Children with very similar family backgrounds often have different abilities, receive different amounts of schooling, and make different choices or confront different opportunities as they mature and enter their adult years. Even siblings raised in the same families often turn out quite differently, a fact that has been used by a number of researchers to study the influence of family environment versus factors external to the family in determining who gets ahead.[2] Some of these other factors, such as education, can be measured and have enabled researchers to explain, at most, 40 to 50 percent of the variation in various measures of adult success.

But this still leaves the glass half empty. Much is not explained by either family background or anything else we can measure. So we are a long way from having a full understanding of why some people succeed and others don't. It could be hard-to-measure qualities such as persistence, social skills, good judgment, or appearance. It could be historical events, such as a war or a depression occurring at a critical juncture in one's life. It could reflect institutional or cultural evaluations that favor some attributes (e.g., having white skin or being a good athlete) over others. Or it could be just plain luck.[3]

Still, family background is at least as important to later success as anything else that can be measured, with the possible exception of education (which is indirectly affected by background in any case).[4] What is it about family background that explains its importance for later success?

Why Is Family Background Important?

Of the many possible reasons for the importance of family background, we focus on three: genetic inheritance, material resources, and a good home environment. In other words, we suspect that higher-income parents may produce more-successful children because they are more able, because they invest more money in their children, and because they are better parents.

A full-scale review of any one of these three topics could fill an entire book. We report some suggestive findings here, as a guide to understanding these extremely important issues. In the absence of such understanding, public policies aimed at improving opportunities for less-advantaged children are likely to produce disappointing results. If genetics are all-important, for example, public policy can do little to affect the degree of inequality other than to redistribute income after the fact. If material resources are crucial, it will help to provide the less advantaged with more money. If home environment is critical, greater efforts to ensure responsible childbearing and good parenting are in order.

GENETIC INHERITANCE

One frequent explanation for the importance of family background is that successful parents pass on good genes to their children. We know that individuals who share the same or similar genes (because they are identical twins or biologically related in some other way) are more similar in terms of their intelligence, sociability, health, and other characteristics than individuals who are not related to each other—even when these individuals have been separated since birth and have experienced quite different environments. For example, children who are adopted end up with educations far more similar to their biological parents' than to those of their adoptive parents. Similarly, identical twins who have been raised apart and may never have known each other share many of the same characteristics.[5]

Of all the characteristics that matter for success, the genetic transmission of cognitive ability—or "intelligence"—has received the most attention. In their controversial and much discussed book, *The Bell Curve*, Richard Herrnstein and Charles Murray suggest that as much as 40 to 80 percent of differences in IQ across individuals are genetically based.[6] Moreover, they suggest that cognitive ability is a critical determinant of economic success and that its importance has increased as society has become more complex and the economy more technologically advanced. They believe we are moving toward a society which is increasingly stratified by intellectual ability, one in which the cognitively elite will receive the greatest rewards and the cognitively disadvantaged the fewest.

Both the substance and the implications of the Herrnstein-Murray argument have been questioned by other researchers. Some researchers argue that they overstate the extent to which ability is inherited, and suggest that a more accurate reading of the evidence on this question may be that 35 to 45 percent of IQ differences across individuals are related in some way to genetic factors.[7] Others cite evidence to support a larger role for genetics.[8] In the end, the importance of genetics in determining individual IQ remains an unresolved and intensely debated topic.

Lower estimates of the genetic component reflect the important interaction between "nature" and "nurture" in determining intelligence. There is evidence that IQ is malleable, with one of the most striking illustrations of this being the so-called "Flynn effect." James R. Flynn found that average IQ scores have been increasing—often dramatically—in every industrialized country for which data are available.[9] Because the gene pool cannot change nearly as quickly as scores have increased throughout this century, the Flynn effect suggests that some significant component of cognitive ability must be shaped by environmental factors.

Whatever the proportion of IQ differences that is in fact genetically based, most research agrees that differences in educational attainment and other environmental factors are more important than IQ or test score differences in determining individual economic outcomes.[10] Recent estimates suggest that no more than 10 to 15 percent of differences in earnings or income is associated with differences in cognitive ability.[11] Still, it seems clear that some significant component of IQ is inherited, that this inherited advantage (or disadvantage) is one of the attributes parents pass on to their children, and that it has some effect on future success. When Thomas Jefferson wrote that "all men are created equal," he was expressing a political statement, not a scientific fact.

MATERIAL RESOURCES

Another possible explanation for the relationship between family background and economic success is that children from low-income families fare poorly because their parents lack the income to provide them with what money can buy—food and clothing, good schools, adequate health care, and housing in a safe neighborhood. In addition, lack of resources may create a stressful environment for the parent, leading to inadequate parenting and poor outcomes for the child.

Many studies find a link between family income during child-hood and later measures of success during adolescence or adult life. For example, children from poor families are twice as like-ly as those from nonpoor families to drop out of high school, to repeat a grade, to be expelled or suspended from school, and to be "economically inactive" in their early 20s (not employed, in school, or taking care of preschool children). As adolescents, they are more likely to bear a child out of wedlock, to commit a crime, and to engage in other risky behaviors.[12] These correlations are frequently used to conclude that low income causes undesirable outcomes among children from poor families. But these correlations do not prove that low income *causes* poor outcomes any more than the World Series occurring in the fall proves that baseball causes cold weather.

To get around the problem of causation, researchers often control for the influence of other factors that may affect adult success but may also be correlated with income. One recent and very ambitious effort of this sort, led by Greg Duncan and Jeanne Brooks-Gunn, involved 13 different research teams, using different data and focusing on different child and adult outcomes but within a consistent analytical framework. Each team looked at the question of how much difference income makes. Their answers varied in size of effect but were consistent in suggesting that—even after controlling for parental education, family structure, and various demographic characteristics—living in poverty, especially persistent poverty, has an effect on later outcomes, especially on children's intellectual achievements when they are young (ages two through eight).[13] Fewer effects were found for older children, for adults, or for behavioral or health outcomes. In a slightly earlier but extreme-ly comprehensive review of the literature, Robert Haveman and Barbara Wolfe noted that a 10 percent increase in parental income typically increases a child's adult earnings by between 1 and 3 percent, even after controlling for other variables.[14]

Even these carefully controlled studies may exaggerate the true effect of material resources on child outcomes, since income often serves as a marker for something else within a family—

something that cannot be measured, and thus controlled for, using existing data but which is equally or more important to the welfare of children. Some of the same characteristics that enable adults to achieve success in the labor market and earn more income may also contribute to their being good parents. These difficult-to-measure characteristics could include their own intelligence, attitudes and values, diligence, good health, sense of responsibility, emotional maturity, parenting methods, and so forth.[15]

The general point, that income may be a marker for something else, has been especially well made by Susan Mayer,[16] who has used a variety of creative analytic techniques to ferret out the extent to which income is associated with better outcomes for children, because it is telling us something about their parents' unobserved characteristics rather than because it is having a direct impact on the welfare of children. She concludes that money does matter somewhat in determining child outcomes, but not nearly as much as most researchers have assumed. It has a small effect on each of a wide range of outcomes, but even a significant increase in the incomes of poor families (like a *doubling* of income for those in the bottom 20 percent of the income distribution) would result in only slight improvements in such later outcomes as educational attainment, dropping out of high school, and becoming pregnant as a teen.

Does this mean the nation can safely eliminate welfare and other parts of the safety net with no consequences? The answer is almost certainly no. For one thing, the research is quite clear that increasing the incomes of children in families below the poverty line has a bigger impact than increasing it for those higher up the income scale.[17] In large part, this is probably because parents with very limited incomes lead extremely stressful lives, may be depressed, and may take out some of their frustrations on their children.[18] Further, current safety net programs effectively protect most families from the kind of serious material hardship that might otherwise interfere with healthy child development—most poor children do get the basic necessities most of the time. It is not clear how generous this safety net needs to be to prevent damage to the next generation. One could easily argue, for example, that until a guarantee of adequate health care exists, children from lower-income families will remain at risk of poor health with all its attendant consequences. Mayer does find, however, that despite already wide variation across states in the size of the safety net, there are no clearly detectable effects on the next generation.

In short, whatever its other merits, it is doubtful that any politically feasible increase in the material resources provided to parents would appreciably change the life trajectories of their children. Mayer's research is hardly the last word on this topic, of course, but it should caution us against assuming that the inheritance of social position in our society is primarily a story about what money can buy.

From a policy perspective, the important point here is that providing greater income transfers to poor families without changing their other characteristics will not necessarily break the link between poverty in one generation and poverty in the next. It may be the right thing to do—as a simple matter of fairness—but it is not likely to transform future lives.

PARENTING AND HOME ENVIRONMENT[19]

As a child grows up, parents do much more, of course, than simply provide material resources. Good parents provide an appropriate mix of warmth and discipline. This is often referred to in the literature as "authoritative" parenting and is usually contrasted to two other styles, overly "permissive" and overly strict or "authoritarian" parenting. Good parenting is not just an abstraction. It has been found to produce better-adjusted and more-successful children.[20] In addition to warmth and discipline, good parents also tend to provide their children with intellectual stimulation (such as reading materials in the home), strong values, and a growing network of connections outside the family—all of which may also contribute to their success.

None of this would matter if good parenting and a stimulating home environment were randomly distributed across the population. But they are not. Most studies have shown that good parenting and a positive home environment often go hand in hand with higher levels of parental income and education.[21]

Further, the structure of the family itself has a significant effect on children's outcomes. Children who grow up with only one biological parent are less successful, on average, than children who grow up living with both parents. This is true across a broad range of outcomes, including labor market success as an adult. And these effects can be found even in families with similar levels of income. In fact, the effects of family structure on various outcomes seem to be due partly to the typically lower incomes in such families and partly to the absence of the second parent, with the two effects being roughly comparable in size.[22] Because about 40 percent of all children now live apart from one parent, up from 12 percent in 1960, the effects of this factor have likely increased.

Thus, some significant component of the effect of family background on success can be explained by factors that take place within the home itself. Disadvantaged children are less likely to experience desirable forms of parenting, to have access to learning experiences that are vital to their early cognitive development, and to grow up in a two-parent family. Overall, differences in parenting practices, home learning environment, and family structure across different family income groups may account for something like one-third to one-half of the overall relationship between family income and children's development.[23] Given the difficulty of measuring such intangibles as "good parenting," these and other figures from the literature are probably lower-bound estimates of the importance of home environment.

CONCLUSION

Genetic inheritance, material resources, and home environment are all correlated with family background and help to explain why it is a strong predictor of later success. The existing literature has not adequately sorted out their relative importance and leaves much unexplained. However, the evidence at least suggests that genetic factors and material resources account for a small part of the association between family background and later success. Home environment (including parenting practices, access to learning experiences, and family structure) appears to play a larger role. However, the three cluster in ways that make distinguishing their separate effects difficult. A single parent who is a high school dropout with few resources—and who out of frustration, despair, or ignorance mistreats or neglects her children—is a case in point. Providing her with additional resources would make her job as a mother easier, but it cannot replace an absent father or guarantee that she will know what to do as a parent to ensure a better future for her children.

NOTES

1. See, e.g., Christopher Jencks et al., *Who Gets Ahead? The Determinants of Economic Success in America* (New York: Basic Books, 1979), 292; Robert Haveman, *Poverty Policy and Poverty Research: The Great Society and the Social Sciences* (Madison, Wis.: University of Wisconsin Press, 1987), 114–116; Robert Haveman and Barbara Wolfe, "The Determinants of Children's Attainments: A Review of Methods and Findings," *Journal of Economic Literature* 33:1829–1878 (December 1995); Robert M. Hauser and Megan M. Sweeney, "Does Poverty in Adolescence Affect the Life Chances of High School Graduates," ed. Greg J. Duncan and Jeanne Brooks-Gunn, *Consequences of Growing Up Poor* (New York: Russell Sage Foundation, 1997), 585.

2. Jencks et al. (1979); Gary Solon et al., "A Longitudinal Analysis of Sibling Correlations in Economic Status," *Journal of Human Resources* 26:509–534 (Summer 1991).

3. See, e.g., Christopher Jencks et al., *Inequality: A Reassessment of the Effect of Family and Schooling in America* (New York: Basic Books, 1972).

4. The relative impact of family background versus education depends on how well family background is measured, but when one includes in family background hard-to-measure influences that affect siblings similarly, the role of background looms at least at large as that of education. For further discussion and some evidence, see Jencks et al. (1979), 10, 214. The best recent reviews of the literature can be found in Haveman and Wolfe (1995) and Duncan and Brooks-Gunn (1997).

5. Edward F. Zigler and Matia Finn Stevenson, *Children in a Changing World: Development and Social Issues*, second edition (Pacific Grove, Calif.: Brooks/Cole Publishing Company, 1993), 105–112.

6. Richard Herrnstein and Charles Murray, *The Bell Curve: Intelligence and Class Structure in American Life* (New York: Free Press, 1994).

7. Bernie Devlin et al., "Galton Redux: Eugenics, Intelligence, Race, and Society: A Review of *The Bell Curve: Intelligence and Class Structure in American Life*," *Journal of the American Statistical Association,* 1483–1488 (1995).

8. Zigler and Stevenson (1993), 105–106.

9. Data for 20 industrialized countries suggest that IQ scores have been rising at a rate of about 15 points (or one standard deviation) per generation. James R. Flynn, "IQ Trends over Time: Intelligence, Race, and Meritocracy," *Meritocracy and Equality,* ed. Steven Durlauf (Princeton, N.J.: Princeton University Press, forthcoming).

10. Claude S. Fischer et al., *Inequality by Design: Cracking the Bell Curve Myth* (Princeton, N.J.: Princeton University Press, 1996), 84–86.

11. William Dickens, Thomas J. Kane, and Charles Schultze, *Does the Bell Curve Ring True? A Reconsideration* (Washington, D.C.: Brookings Institution, forthcoming); and McKinley L. Blackburn and David Neumark, "Omitted-Ability Bias and the Increase in Return to Schooling," *Journal of Labor Economics* 11:521–544 (1993). Similar results are reported using 1962 data in Jencks et al. (1972).

12. Jeanne Brooks-Gunn and Greg J. Duncan, "The Effects of Poverty on Children," Center for the Future of Children, The David and Lucile Packard Foundation, *The Future of Children* 7:58–59 (summer/fall 1997).

13. Greg J. Duncan and Jeanne Brooks-Gunn, "Income Effects across the Life Span: Integration and Interpretation," *Consequences of Growing Up Poor,* ed. Greg J. Duncan and Jeanne Brooks-Gunn (New York: Russell Sage Foundation, 1997).

14. Haveman and Wolfe (1995), 1864.

15. Duncan and Brooks-Gunn (1997), 601. Duncan and Brooks-Gunn appear to believe that the quality of the home environment—including the quality of mother-child interactions, the physical condition of the home, and opportunities to learn—is responsible for a substantial portion of the effects of income on cognitive outcomes. And although providing such things as educational toys, reading materials, or a safe play area can cost money, they are not necessarily large items in most family budgets.

16. Susan E. Mayer, *What Money Can't Buy: Family Income and Children's Life Chances* (Cambridge, Mass.: Harvard University Press, 1997).

17. Duncan and Brooks-Gunn (1997), 597. John Shea, "Does Parents' Money Matter?" Working paper 6026 (Cambridge, Mass.: National Bureau of Economic Research, Inc., May 1997).

18. Rand Conger et al., "A Family Process Model of Economic Hardship and Adjustment of Early Adolescent Boys," *Child Development* 63:526–541 (1992).

19. We are indebted to Deborah Phillips (Board on Children, Youth, and Families; Institute of Medicine; National Research Council) and Edward Zigler (Yale University) for their assistance in guiding us through some of the relevant literature on this topic.

20. This typology was developed by Diana Baumrind, who showed, in a series of studies, that parenting practices are a major influence on child development (Zigler and Stevenson [1993], 373). Also see Eleanor Maccoby, "Socialization in the Context of the Family: Parent-Child Interaction," *Handbook of Child Psychology,* ed. Paul H. Mussen (New York: John Wiley and Son, 1983), 39–51.

21. For further discussion and cites to the literature, see Thomas L. Hanson, Sara McLanahan, and Elizabeth Thomson, "Economic Resources, Parental Practices, and Children's Well-Being," in Duncan and Brooks-Gunn (1997), 190–238. These authors find that household income and debt are only weakly related to effective parenting, but note that "our results differ from those of other studies," which find stronger effects. The differences may relate to the peculiarities of the data used for this one study. Also see endnote 23.

22. Sara McLanahan, "Parent Absence or Poverty: Which Matters More?" in Duncan and Brooks-Gunn (1997), 35–48.

23. Duncan and Brooks-Gunn (1997) find that the home learning environment alone can explain up to one-third of the overall relationship.

Chapter Ten

Policy Implications and a Look at the Future

O ur primary purpose in this volume has been to understand why some people succeed over the course of their lives and others do not. Exploring in detail what policy measures could bring us closer to achieving the American ideal of equal opportunity is a task for yet another volume. However, we do wish to suggest some directions for public and private action and take a brief look into the future.

POLICY IMPLICATIONS

Education

At the top of our list we would put improving the public schools. As emphasized in chapters 2 and 6, the broadening of educational opportunities earlier in the nation's history appears to have reduced the influence of class or social origins on later success, but we are less sanguine about the future. Changes in the family—such as more single parents and more working mothers—have fragmented families and put additional burdens on schools. A changing economy has increased the demand for skilled workers. This, in combination with the failure of the public schools to satisfy this demand, has increased the value of a college education but also its cost—further skewing opportunities toward those most able to pay. In our view, the solution is not more subsidies for higher education. This might only serve to further inflate the price. Rather, it is to improve precollege training so that more people can qualify for good jobs with or without a college degree. Improving precollege training requires parallel actions along two tracks: distributing school resources more equally, and using those resources more effectively to produce positive educational outcomes.

A more equal distribution of school resources requires that the current system of school finance be fundamentally changed. It is ironic that a nation placing so much emphasis on equal opportunity should end up delegating virtually all funding of public education to local communities. One would have expected that such a country—which guarantees income and health care to the elderly—would also guarantee a good education to each of its children, regardless of where they live. In the long run, a much larger federal role in evening out fiscal disparities could be combined with more local competition and accountability to ensure that such funds are used effectively.

Legal challenges in state courts have had some success in bringing about a more equitable distribution of school resources. In particular, in the 13 states in which courts ordered reforms to the school finance system between 1973 and 1993, spending inequality within those states was reduced by between 16 and 38 percent following the reform. This was achieved through increases in state aid to the poorest districts, as aid to the wealthiest districts remained generally constant in those states.[1] But because of its case-by-case nature, state litigation does not represent a comprehensive solution to the problem of school resource inequality. Further, because interdistrict inequality within a given state represents only about one-third of the overall inequality in the national distribution of school resources (two-thirds results from differences between states), much of the inequality remains beyond the reach of even successful state litigation. Thus, any broad effort to reduce school finance inequality would require involvement of the federal government.

In fact, there have been recent legislative efforts to improve the targeting of available federal resources under the Title I compensatory education program. The effect, however, has been minimal, increasing the amount of federal Title I funds received by the poorest counties by only about 1 to 3 percent. The 1994 revision of the Elementary and Secondary Education Act (ESEA) created a new federal financial incentive for states to create more-equitable systems of school finance, but no funds have been appropriated for it.[2]

Improving effectiveness requires changes both inside and outside individual schools. One reasonable first step for school improvement would be to increase the dissemination and use of certain models designed to improve student performance—especially the performance of less-advantaged students. One model, called "Success for All," has produced large effects, with students in participating schools being a year ahead of those in a matched set of nonparticipating schools by fifth grade.[3]

Changes in other areas must complement reforms inside the schools. These include incentives that reward students for strong performance on an individual basis. Standards-based systems and voluntary national tests that enable students to demonstrate their achievements and provide feedback to schools and parents have much to recommend them in this respect. Some form of financial incentive contingent on performance on such a test— such as a college tuition tax credit—would create an additional incentive to succeed.

These reforms have been attacked from both sides of the political spectrum. Conservatives tend to oppose anything that undermines local control of the schools. But without a national consensus on what children should be expected to learn, some way of knowing what they have actually learned, and national incentives for high performance for both schools and students, there will be no way to shake the current complacency of many school systems. Liberals, for their part, tend to oppose high-stakes testing for fear it will harm the very children whose initial educational disadvantages are the greatest, especially minorities and the poor. But this view ignores the terrible injustice of leaving the fate of these children to the exigencies of family background, which will always be the dominant influence on who gets ahead as long as the education system is relatively weak.

Early Childhood Education and Support for Families

As noted in chapter 9, children from more-disadvantaged backgrounds tend to begin school with various social and cognitive deficits that could be ameliorated by investments in their early education and care. Many such efforts already exist—from Head Start to preschool programs funded by states—and not all have been successful. Moreover, the most intensive, high-quality programs that appear to produce the best results are often expensive. For example, the much-touted Perry Preschool Project would cost over $7,000 per child annually in today's dollars. But both formal evaluations and informed opinion suggest that the long-term benefits outweigh the costs. Although short-term gains in IQ or cognitive ability often fade over time, the programs typically improve a number of other measures of school success, including high school graduation.[4]

Most of the programs do not begin until a child is three or four. Even earlier interventions may be needed. New evidence suggests that the brain develops most rapidly during the first few years of life, that the environment plays a greater role than earlier suspected in affecting that development, and that the effects can be long lasting.[5] And model programs that begin during infancy often show larger gains than those that start later.[6] A new "Early Head Start" that would serve children under age three was established in 1994 but with extremely limited funding.

Not only do such programs need to start early to be most effective, they also need to be combined with continuing compensatory efforts once children are in school. It should not be assumed that a good preschool experience can inoculate children against an inadequate learning environment once they enroll in the primary grades. It is for this reason, among others, that we believe more attention to the basic K through 12 education system is so important.

Another appealing approach to reducing cognitive and social deficits among children from less-advantaged families is to help their parents to provide better and more-stimulating home environments. This has led a number of states as well as the federal government to launch what are often called "family support" or parenting education programs. Thus far, however, programs that attempt to change children's lives by first changing their parents have not proven to be as effective as direct investments in early childhood education.[7] The two need not be mutually exclusive, of course, and it may be possible to kill two birds with one stone by involving parents as child care aides in Head Start or other preschool programs, or by adding a home visiting component to such programs.

Affirmative Action

We have touched only lightly on the extent to which opportunities vary by race, gender, or ethnicity. But we have been struck by the fact that progress on these fronts has been greater than it has been in reducing the impediments of class. Both African Americans and women have made dramatic gains over the past 30 years. If you want to predict how well a child born in the United States in 1998 will do in the future, it is more important to know his or her parents' socioeconomic status than it is to know his or her race or gender. This was not always true.

We are not arguing against affirmative action, but we do want to suggest that its relevance seems increasingly marginal. No amount of affirmative action is going to guarantee African American children who are born into poor families and attend poor schools a secure place in the job market of the future. Efforts to remedy past wrongs and to diversify institutions are commendable—but it would be a serious mistake, we think, to rely on yesterday's weapons to win tomorrow's wars.

Taxes, Government Benefits, and the Welfare System

Growing income inequality leads naturally to a concern about the distributional effects of current taxes and benefit programs for poor families, such as Food Stamps, housing or medical assistance, and cash welfare. These have served to moderate the inequality of market outcomes. However, recent policy actions, such as the 1996 welfare bill and the 1997 budget bill, have been regressive in their impact, further exacerbating the widening gap between the rich and the poor.

Our own preference would be for a more equal distribution of income. But this preference rests mostly on our desire to live in a society in which extremes of income and wealth do not exist, rather than on any sense that this would greatly enhance opportunity or substantially change the life trajectories of today's children.

As emphasized in chapter 9, we see little evidence that material poverty is the major reason for the poor outcomes experienced by so many children in low-income families. However, this may be because the United States has already succeeded in eliminating many of the worst forms of material deprivation. The value of a basic safety net that places a floor below which people are not permitted to sink—that keeps them fed, clothed, housed, and relatively healthy—is not much in question, although exactly how much protection it should afford is another matter. The fact that this floor varies widely from state to state illustrates the difficulty. This unhappy anomaly existed long before welfare was reformed and more policy discretion was given to the states. However, the termination of matching grants from the federal government creates new fiscal incentives for the states that will almost inevitably increase these geographic disparities in the reach and generosity of the safety net. States with the lowest benefit levels stand to gain the most from cutbacks in their own spending.[8]

In addition to its impact on the safety net, welfare reform has other implications. As this book goes to press, welfare caseloads are declining, leading some to hail reform as a great success. We would like to suggest two other criteria for evaluating its effects.

The first is the ability of current recipients to achieve self-sufficiency and later move up the economic ladder. What little evidence we have suggests that many recipients—when pushed—will find jobs. But they will have much greater difficulty making ends meet and moving into higher-paid work. This underscores the importance of providing greater supports for the so-called working poor—in the form of subsidized child care, health insurance, and the Earned Income Tax Credit.

Our second concern is the future of children in such families. Will their prospects be diminished or improved? This question is especially difficult to answer, depending as it does on the quality of substitute care compared to what mothers may now be providing, on the impact of work on mothers' relationships with their children, and on the effects of the new system on future childbearing decisions, especially among unwed teens. All these effects could well be positive if good-quality child care is available, if work improves these mothers' self-image without putting them under undue stress as parents, and if welfare is no longer viewed as a long-term source of support for those who bear children before they are ready to support them. Whether these prove to be true remains to be seen. But, at a minimum, the nation should not miss the opportunity to provide good-quality care to the children of welfare recipients while they are working—especially since there is evidence suggesting that good out-of-home care can have positive benefits for children from low-income families.[9]

PROSPECTS FOR THE FUTURE[10]

Taken together, the facts we have reviewed in the preceding nine chapters have strong implications for future social mobility and for America's ability to retain its historic commitment to opportunity. Because mobility depends on growth, future generations are going to experience less of it unless the economy moves back onto a faster growth path. Because mobility depends increasingly on education, those who fail to get a good education are more and more at risk of becoming marginalized. And because mobility depends on family environment, and families are under new stresses, a growing number of children face diminished life chances for this reason as well.

What are the chances that these trends will be reversed?

One possibility is that productivity growth will improve. Corporate downsizing, the restructuring of the economy in response to international competition, the opening of new markets abroad, the information revolution, and the commitment to reduce the deficit could all contribute to this result. Thus far, however, productivity growth, as conventionally measured, has not improved.

Another possibility is that there will be a supply-side response to the growing premium paid to well-educated workers. For example, as it becomes clear that the best way to get ahead is to attend college, more and more people may make this investment in their own futures—aided perhaps by the less costly, easier-to-repay student loans introduced in 1993 and the tax subsidies and enhanced Pell grants enacted in 1997. As this occurs, it should narrow the differential in earnings paid to those with different levels of skill. But, as we have stressed repeatedly, without public and private efforts designed to improve elementary and secondary schools, more college-going will not necessarily improve opportunity, since universities are at the level of the education system that is most stratified by class.

Finally, there is some evidence of a new public yearning for more-stable families, as well as a new receptivity to attitudes and values that could, in time, produce more-responsible parenting and better environments for children. Current estimates are that almost half of all first births in the United States are to mothers who are either teenagers, unmarried, or lacking a high school degree.[11] These are high-risk environments for children, as noted in chapter 9, and do not auger well for their futures. Those who believe that such public policies as denying welfare benefits to unwed mothers will stem the rise of out-of-wedlock childbearing in any direct way are, according to the evidence, likely to be disappointed. But the message they are sending may eventually affect societal attitudes and thus behavior more indirectly. In the meantime society would seem to have little choice but to invest more in the health, education, and socialization of young children in an attempt to compensate for what they do not receive at home. But those who believe that such programs can significantly reduce poverty among children tend to forget how small these investments are, and probably always will be, relative to the need. (Federal and state spending on early child-hood education is estimated at around $10 billion annually. This contrasts to the $318 billion spent on elementary and secondary education.) We can welcome and encourage additional investments while remaining skeptical about their ability to fully compensate for what families may not provide.

What happens if these trends do not reverse—if productivity growth remains sluggish, if a large proportion of the population fails to upgrade their skills, and if families continue to fragment? In this case, a diminution of upward mobility seems almost inevitable. And since no one wants to accept this result, the debate is likely to revolve around how, not whether, to reverse the trend and the role that government versus families should play in these efforts.

* * * * *

Liberals argue that government should become more heavily involved in providing an equal chance for children and want more money spent on social services, income assistance, education, and jobs. Conservatives argue that government programs cannot address, and may even undermine, the stability of the family and the values of self-reliance and hard work that have been critical ingredients in the success stories of immigrants and previous generations of Americans.

We would argue that there is truth in both propositions and that to restore a sense of opportunity the country needs a new generation of policies that recognizes this more complex understanding. The debate has been about growth versus fairness, about the role of markets versus the role of government, about culture versus economics, and about what we should do as individuals versus what we should do as a community. Finding the right balance between these is what democratic discourse is all about. Honoring the now-tarnished, but still very American, idea of opportunity is one way to strike that balance.

NOTES

1. William N. Evans, Sheila E. Murray, and Robert M. Schwab, "Schoolhouses, Courthouses, and Statehouses after *Serrano*," *Journal of Policy Analysis and Management* 16:10–31 (1997).

2. For a more detailed discussion of this provision of the law, see Wayne Riddle, "Education for the Disadvantaged: Analysis of 1994 ESEA Title I Allocation Formula Amendments," *Journal of Education Finance* 21:217–235 (1995).

3. For a summary of the research on "Success for All," "Accelerated Learning," and the "School Development Program," see W. Steven Barnett, "Economics of School Reform: Three Promising Models," *Holding Schools Accountable,* ed. Helen F. Ladd (Washington, D.C.: Brookings Institution, 1996), 327–356.

4. The David and Lucile Packard Foundation, "Long-Term Outcomes of Early Childhood Programs," *The Future of Children* 5 (winter 1995). See especially the articles by Deanna S. Gomby et al. and W. Steven Barnett.

5. Carnegie Corporation of New York, *Starting Points: Meeting the Needs of Our Youngest Children* (1994), 6–8.

6. Packard Foundation (1995), 35.

7. Ibid., 16.

8. Poorer states that typically pay low benefits used to face the prospect of losing more than $4 in federal funds for every $1 by which they cut their own spending, whereas richer states that cut spending by the same $1 lost far less—closer to $2. Now rich and poor states are on an equal footing. A dollar saved is roughly a dollar saved, creating new incentives for the poorer states to reduce their already meager benefits.

9. One recent study found that child care during the preschool years affected reading and math scores at ages five and six but quite differently depending on whether the children were from high- or low-income homes. The effects were positive for low-income children but negative for their more-advantaged counterparts. See Packard Foundation (1995), 27.

10. This section draws heavily on Isabel V. Sawhill, "Opportunity in America," *Opportunity in the United States: Social and Individual Responsibility* (Washington, D.C.: The Aspen Institute, 1996).

11. Nicholas Zill and Christine W. Nord, "Running in Place" (Washington, D.C.: Child Trends, Inc., 1994).

higher, 18, 21–22n.14, 33–34,
35, 42, 48, 49, 61, 66–69,
69n.2, 72n.20, 85–86
income and, 8, 18
inherited abilities and, 4–5,
27–28
law and legislation, 86–87
mobility and, 8, 33–34, 35
occupations and, 48, 49
opportunities and, 10–12,
17–18, 27–28, 49, 62–63
outcomes, 65, 70n.14
parental, 63
performance measures, 65
per-pupil expenditures, 64–65,
70n.13, 70n.14, 71n.15
provision of, 11–12
public assistance and, 11–12
public policy, 85–89
reforms, 87
school resources, 62–63, 65, 86
secondary, 62–63, 87
social class and, 4–5, 27–28,
67–69, 69n.6
student-teacher ratios, 65,
71n.15
support of, 18
EITC. *see* Earned Income Tax
Credit (EITC)
Elementary and Secondary
Education Act of 1994, 87
Employment
expenses of, 56, 59n.14, 59n.15
job growth, 51–52, 57n.2
opportunities for, 51
unskilled workers, 54
upward mobility and, 56–57
welfare recipients, 51, 52–54,
56–57, 57–58n.4, 58n.5,
58n.6, 60
Europe, 28

F

Fairness test, 24, 25–27

Families
child outcomes, 78, 79–80,
83n.21
effect of opportunity on, 19
generational income
relationship, 46–47, 50n.3
genetic inheritance and, 74–76
home environment, 79–80,
82n.15, 83n.21, 83n.23
importance of, 73–76, 81n.4
income-education
relationship, 67
material resources, 76–79,
82n.15
parenting and, 79–80, 83n.20
single-parent, 19, 59n.15, 80, 81
social justice and, 27–29
values in, 25
wages and, 39, 43n.3, 43n.4
see also Socioeconomic status
Featherman, David, 69n.6
Fertility, 50n.11
Flynn, James R., 76, 82n.9

G

Gender issues
affirmative action, 13, 89
employment opportunities, 19,
22n.19
income, 4, 22n.19, 39–40, 43n.4
opportunities and, 16–17,
22n.19
role in mobility, 8
Genetic inheritance, 74–76

H

Hanson, Thomas L., 83n.21,
83n.23
Haveman, Robert, 3–4, 77
Head Start, 5, 88–89
Herrnstein, Richard, 4, 28, 30n.13,
75–76
Home environment, 79–80,
83n.21, 83n.23, 92

genetic inheritance and, 74–76
home environment and, 79–80,
82n.15, 83n.21, 83n.23
importance of, 73–76, 81n.4
income and, 4
material resources, 76–79,
82n.15
opportunities and, 61
parenting and, 79–80, 83n.20
role in mobility, 8–9
see also Underclass
Standardized tests, 63, 70n.14
Success for All, 87

T

Technology advances, 42–43, 66
Tocqueville, Alexis de, 16, 21n.4
Turner, Frederick Jackson, 17

U

Underclass, 9–10
see also Disadvantaged groups
Unemployment, 51–52, 57n.3
Unemployment insurance, 58n.5
Upward mobility, 10, 17, 33–34,
48–49, 50n.11, 56–57, 62

W

Wages. *see* Income
Welfare. *see* Public assistance
Welfare reform, 52–54, 56–57, 60,
90–91
Will, George, 23
Wills, Garry, 28
Wilson, James Q., 24
Wolfe, Barbara, 77
World War II, post-war period, 7,
20, 31, 40, 42

About the Authors

Daniel P. McMurrer is a senior researcher at the American Society for Training and Development in Alexandria, Virginia, where his research focuses on the effects of human capital investments such as training and workplace education. Prior to this, Mr. McMurrer was a research associate at the Urban Institute, where he co-wrote and co-edited the Institute's *Opportunity in America* policy brief series with Isabel V. Sawhill. Before joining the Urban Institute, Mr. McMurrer was a social science research analyst at the federal Advisory Council on Unemployment Compensation.

Isabel V. Sawhill is a senior fellow in economic studies at the Brookings Institution in Washington, D.C., where she holds the Adeline M. and Alfred I. Johnson chair. Dr. Sawhill was formerly a senior fellow and the first occupant of the Arjay Miller chair in public policy at the Urban Institute. Her previous publications include *Welfare Reform: An Analysis of the Issues; Challenge to Leadership: Economic and Social Issues for the Next Decade;* and *The Reagan Record.* She served as an associate director of the Office of Management and Budget from 1993 to 1995.